SCROLL SAW
BASICS

Patrick Spielman

 Sterling Publishing Co., Inc.   New York

Metric Equivalents

INCHES TO MILLIMETRES AND CENTIMETRES

MM—millimetres   CM—centimetres

Inches	MM	CM	Inches	CM	Inches	CM
⅛	3	0.3	9	22.9	30	76.2
¼	6	0.6	10	25.4	31	78.7
⅜	10	1.0	11	27.9	32	81.3
½	13	1.3	12	30.5	33	83.8
⅝	16	1.6	13	33.0	34	86.4
¾	19	1.9	14	35.6	35	88.9
⅞	22	2.2	15	38.1	36	91.4
1	25	2.5	16	40.6	37	94.0
1¼	32	3.2	17	43.2	38	96.5
1½	38	3.8	18	45.7	39	99.1
1¾	44	4.4	19	48.3	40	101.6
2	51	5.1	20	50.8	41	104.1
2½	64	6.4	21	53.3	42	106.7
2	76	7.6	22	55.9	43	109.2
3½	89	8.9	23	58.4	44	111.8
4	102	10.2	24	61.0	45	114.3
4½	114	11.4	25	63.5	46	116.8
5	127	12.7	26	66.0	47	119.4
6	152	15.2	27	68.6	48	121.9
7	178	17.8	28	71.1	49	124.5
8	203	20.3	29	73.7	50	127.0

Library of Congress Cataloging-in-Publication Data

Spielman, Patrick E.
    Scroll saw basics / Patrick Spielman.
        p.   cm.
    Includes index.
    ISBN 0-8069-7224-6
    1. Woodwork.   2. Jig saws.   I. Title.
    TT180.S646   1991
    684'.083—dc20   90-27669
                                     CIP

1   3   5   7   9   10   8   6   4   2

Copyright © 1991 by Patrick Spielman
Published by Sterling Publishing Company, Inc.
387 Park Avenue South, New York, NY 10016
Distributed in Canada by Sterling Publishing
% Canadian Manda Group, P.O. Box 920, Station U
Toronto, Ontario, Canada M8Z 5P9
Distributed in Great Britain and Europe by Cassell PLC
Villiers House, 41/47 Strand, London WC2N 5JE, England
Distributed in Australia by Capricorn Ltd.
P.O. Box 665, Lane Cove, NSW 2066
Manufactured in the United States of America
All rights reserved

Sterling ISBN 0-8069-7224-6

Contents

ACKNOWLEDGMENTS

My sincere appreciation goes once again to Dirk Boelman, a superb designer and artist who, with the assistance of my daughter, Sherri Valitchka, provided some excellent illustrations and patterns. Many thanks to Julie Kiehnau for her scroll-sawings, for keeping my illustrations in order, and for making the manuscript presentable. I thank my good friend and colleague James Reidle, who allowed me to use some illustrations from books we co-authored, and professional scroller, Mark Berner, for the auxiliary saw table idea. Illustrative or technical help was provided by the following scroll-saw companies: Advanced Machinery Imports Ltd., American Machine and Tool Co., Delta Machinery Corp., Dremel, Excalibur, Heartwood, Jet, Olson Saw Co., Penn State Industries, Reidle Products, R. B. Industries, Sakura U.S.A., Sears, Seyco Sales Co., and Value Craft.

INTRODUCTION

Scroll-sawing is quite possibly the most popular and rewarding of all woodworking activities. There are many reasons for this. The modern scroll saw is very affordable, well-made, and very safe to use. Also, no previous woodworking experience or mechanical or artistic ability is needed to use it successfully. And, due to the simplicity of scroll-saw design, the operator does not need to frequently adjust, tune-up, or provide maintenance for it, as is often required of most other woodworking tools to make them perform safely and efficiently.

In fact, the scroll saw is the easiest power tool to master, and is ideal for beginners. It is also suited for more advanced woodworkers because it can be used for a wide range of techniques, from simple cutouts (Illus. I-1 and I-2) to exquisite fretwork (Illus. I-3) to advanced works of inlay, marquetry, and intarsia, and even cuttings which involve plastics, metals, and other material.

There are other advantages to scroll-sawing. Scroll-sawing requires little work space and creates a minimum amount of waste, dust, and noise. Wood scraps normally too small to be cut safely on other tools can be sawn into useful objects and projects as a matter of routine on the scroll saw. One of the most favorable features of the modern scroll saw is its ability to make incredibly smooth cuts that virtually eliminate the drudgery of sanding.

All scroll-sawing activities are by and large "self-contained" when compared to other categories of woodworking like making furniture and cabinets. Such activities usually require other expensive auxiliary tools and machines that involve much knowledge and skill to operate.

The purpose of this book is to help those unfamiliar with scroll saws understand the basics—the types of scroll saw available and their features, the blades available, and how to make basic cuts

Illus. I-1. *Making country-styled cutouts and wooden letters are just two of many popular scroll-sawing activities. Note the economical bench scroll saw being used to produce these items.*

safely and efficiently. In addition to the illustrated guidelines of techniques and procedures, some full-size, ready-to-use patterns are also included, so that the learning and creating processes can start simultaneously and immediately.

Illus. I-2. *The very narrow blades carried in modern scroll saws are remarkably sturdy for their size. They can be used to cut extremely sharp corners and turns without fear that they will break.*

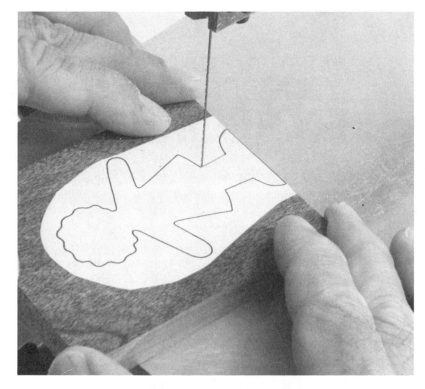

Illus. I-3. *Ornate pieces such as these fretwork projects are well within the capabilities of every scroll-saw user.*

Chapter 1
EXPLORING SCROLL SAWS

The scroll saw is an easy-to-use power tool designed to cut curves in flat wood. (See Illus. 1-1.) It carries a very narrow saw blade that reciprocates—that is, moves with an up-and-down cutting action. The blade actually cuts only on its downward stroke.

Scroll saws are often compared to band saws because both have the capability to make many similar kinds of cuts. There are, however, some very definite differences between the machines. (See Illus. 1-2.) The major performance differences are as follow:

1. The band saw has the capability to saw thicker material, and can generally cut it much faster than the scroll saw. Most scroll saws will, however, cut stock up to 2 inches thick; some can cut stock up to 2¾ inches thick.

2. Scroll saws produce very smooth sawn surfaces which seldom require any sanding. (See Illus. 1-3.) Band saws leave much rougher surfaces that are often difficult or impossible to sand or smooth.

3. Scroll saws carry much narrower blades; these blades can be used to cut sharper curves and make more highly detailed cuts than are possible with a band saw. Cutting inside openings (like the hole in the letter O) is routine on the scroll saw

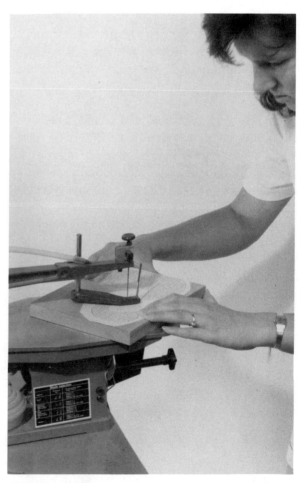

Illus. 1-1. *Unlike most other woodworking machines, scroll saws need virtually no adjustment, alignment, or maintenance.*

Illus. 1-2. The basic mechanical differences between the band saw (left) and the modern constant-tension scroll saw (right). Both are powered by electric motors (not shown), and both have tension applied to their blades. Tension on the band saw is obtained by raising the upper wheel. Tension on the scroll saw is obtained by applying vertical pressure to the arms. The blades are always under uniform ("constant") tension throughout the cutting strokes.

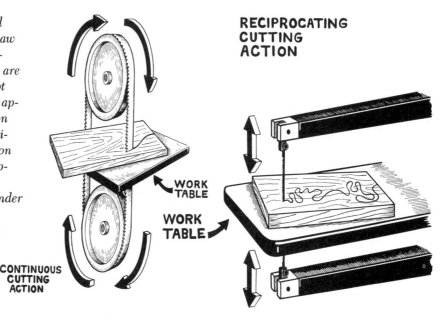

RECIPROCATING CUTTING ACTION

WORK TABLE

WORK TABLE

CONTINUOUS CUTTING ACTION

because its narrow blade can be threaded through a hole drilled in the inside waste area. (See Chapter 9.) It is impossible to saw inside openings with a band saw.

4. Because of their continuous and faster cutting action, band saws require considerably more skill and are, consequently, more dangerous to operate. Should a finger accidentally touch a scroll-saw blade in operation, only a very slight nick might result that probably will not even draw blood. However, such an accident on the band saw is likely to be very serious and traumatic.

5. Scroll saws do not require maintenance or critical adjustments, as do band saws, to make them function properly.

Scroll saws, like band saws, are available in various styles and in different price categories. Scroll saws range in price from under $100 to over $2,000.

Sizes of Scroll Saw

Scroll saws are sized or classified according to four specifications: throat capacity, thickness-cutting capacity, stroke length, and cutting speed. **Throat capacity** is the most commonly used classification. This is the distance from the blade to the rear of the machine. (See Illus. 1-4.) The throat capacities of scroll saws range from 12 to 26 inches. A saw with an 18-inch throat capacity, for example, can

Illus. 1-3. Comparing two sawn surfaces cut from the same piece of oak hardwood. The upper surface was cut with a typical, medium-sized band-saw blade. The lower, smooth surface was cut with a relatively coarse, No. 9 scroll-saw blade.

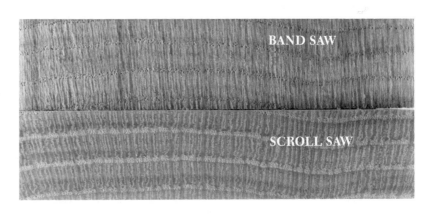

BAND SAW

SCROLL SAW

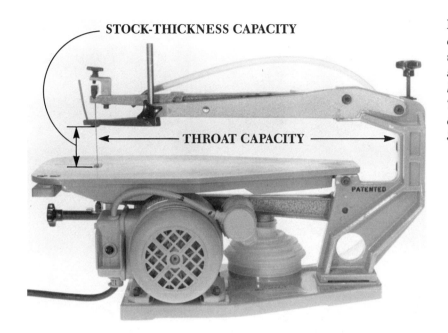

STOCK-THICKNESS CAPACITY

THROAT CAPACITY

Illus. 1-4. *Scroll saws are usually designated by their throat capacity. A saw classified as an 18-inch saw measures 18 inches from the blade to the rear of the machine. This saw can cut to the center of a circular workpiece that measures 36 inches in diameter.*

cut to the center of a 36-inch-diameter circular workpiece.

Thickness capacity is the maximum thickness of wood that the saw can cut. (See Illus. 1-4.) **Stroke length** is the distance the blade moves from the bottom to the top of its reciprocation. Typical stroke lengths range from ⅝ to 1¼ inches. Longer strokes provide cooler, more efficient cutting because they get the sawdust out of the cut more quickly.

The **cutting speed** of a scroll saw is specified as strokes per minute, abbreviated as spm. Certain saws have different cutting speeds. These saws are variable-speed saws. The ability to change cutting speeds to accommodate and control different cutting jobs or to cut various materials efficiently is an important feature to the scroll-saw user.

Types of Scroll Saw

Today, the most popular scroll saws are the "constant-tension" saws. The term constant tension refers to the uninterrupted strain placed on the blade during its cutting process. This strain or tension is mechanically created by the design of

the saw, and is basically a means of stretching or pulling the blade in its length to stiffen it.

There are two different types of constant-tension scroll saw. The most popular type is the "parallel-arm" saw. (See Illus. 1-5.) The second type is the "C-arm" saw. (See Illus. 1-6.)

The oldest and least popular type of scroll saw is the "rigid-arm" saw. (See Illus. 1-7.) The major shortcoming of this type of saw is that by the inherent design of the saw, its blade is not always strained in a constant tension throughout its cutting stroke. The rigid-arm scroll saw, because of its declining popularity, will not be further examined.

Scroll saws may also be categorized as either "bench models" (Illus. 1-8) or as freestanding "floor models" (Illus. 1-9). Some bench saws can be mounted to optional floor stands; other saws, by the nature of their design, can only be placed on their floor stands. (See Illus. 1-5.)

With the exception of the Delta 18-inch C-arm floor-model scroll saw, nearly all the new scroll saws available today are parallel-arm saws. The cutting action provided by a C-arm scroll saw is not as efficient nor as accurate as that of a parallel-arm saw.

Note that the C-arm scroll saw shown in Illus. 1-6 and 1-10 has only one pivot point. The rocking arm style of the C design creates a blade-stroking

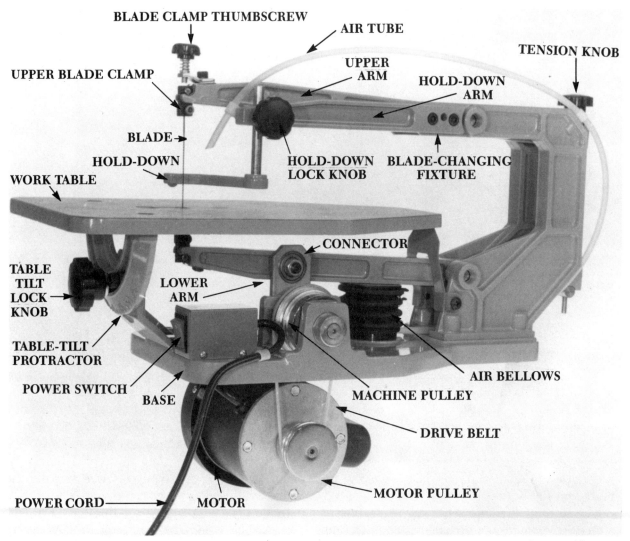

BLADE CLAMP THUMBSCREW

AIR TUBE

TENSION KNOB

UPPER BLADE CLAMP

UPPER ARM

HOLD-DOWN ARM

BLADE→

HOLD-DOWN

HOLD-DOWN LOCK KNOB

BLADE-CHANGING FIXTURE

WORK TABLE

CONNECTOR

TABLE TILT LOCK KNOB

LOWER ARM

TABLE-TILT PROTRACTOR

AIR BELLOWS

POWER SWITCH

BASE

MACHINE PULLEY

DRIVE BELT

POWER CORD

MOTOR

MOTOR PULLEY

Illus. 1-5. *The essential parts of this Sakura 14-inch, three-speed constant-tension scroll saw are fairly representative of most modern scroll saws. This saw, however, requires a special stand, shown in Illus.*

1-9. Note the step pulleys and belt provisions for changing the speed at which the blade reciprocates (moves up and down).

action that is not always perfectly vertical throughout its entire cutting stroke. This is often a problem when thick material is being sawed.

Parallel-arm saws have two pivot points incorporated into an overall parallelogram design that creates a blade-stroking action which is always in a true vertical position. (See Illus. 1-11 and 1-13.) Cuts made with this type of saw will always be perfectly vertical. Since parallel-arm saws have the most popular and most efficient saw design, all further discussions and illustrations will apply only to this type of saw.

Important Parts and Features

Parallel-arm constant-tension saws are fairly similar in their general appearances and operations. Their major differences lie in their overall construction quality, the design of their blade suspension (clamping and support systems), and in their blade-tensioning mechanisms. These features and specific parts are examined in the following pages.

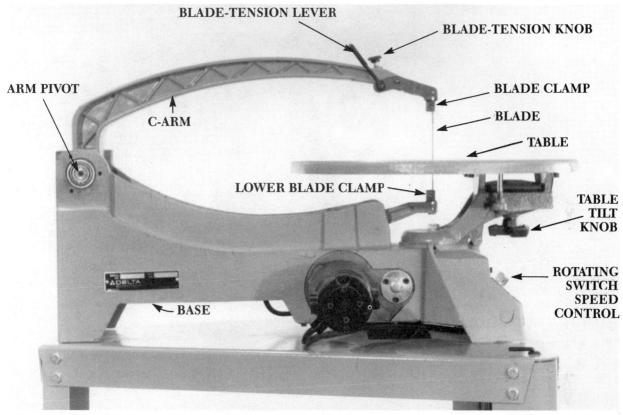

BLADE-TENSION LEVER

BLADE-TENSION KNOB

ARM PIVOT

C-ARM

BLADE CLAMP

BLADE

TABLE

LOWER BLADE CLAMP

TABLE TILT KNOB

ROTATING SWITCH SPEED CONTROL

BASE

Illus. 1-6. *The Delta C-arm saw. Here, the upper and lower arms are connected in a one-piece, cast-C configuration. Note the single pivot typical only of this style of saw.*

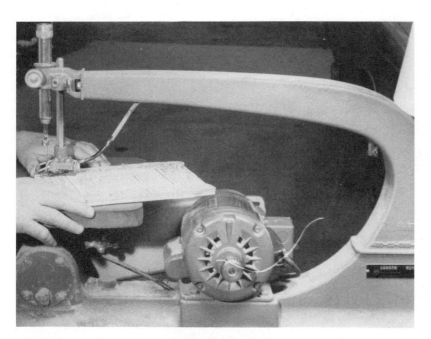

Illus. 1-7. *A rigid-arm saw is commonly called a jigsaw. A spring mechanism located on the forward end of the stationary overarm pulls the blade upward for its upstroke. Because of its design and the fact that it does not perform well, this type of saw is not as popular as constant-tension saws.*

Illus. 1-8. *This bench-model parallel-arm scroll saw from AMT has a 23-inch throat capacity.*

Arms

The *arms* of the saws provide support for the blade clamps on their forward ends. The blade-tensioning system on most saws is to the rear of the arm's pivot points. (See Illus. 1-11 and 1-13.) The arm supports are usually made of cast aluminum or cast iron and are connected in some way (usually by bolts) to the machine base.

Base

The *base* supports the upper structure of the scroll saw. Design differences can be found in the bases of parallel-arm constant-tension saws. Some bases are made of formed sheet steel and are an integral part of the supporting stand. (See Illus. 1-11.) Others are made of cast iron or aluminum (Illus. 1-5) and rest independently on a bench or stand (Illus. 1-8 and 1-9).

Tables

The *tables* are usually made of aluminum or cast iron. They support the workpiece during cutting. Most saws have tilting tables to permit bevel cuts. Bevel-sawing is making cuts that are at angles to the thickness of the wood.

The designs of the *table slots* and *table openings* vary among manufacturers. Some slots extend from the blade opening all the way forward through the front edge of the table. This style is preferred by the author over partial slots that terminate before exiting out of the front table edge.

Illus. 1-9 (left). *The 14½-inch Hegner Multimax 14 and the Sakura 14-inch parallel-arm scroll saws on stands. Note the comparative floor space required.*

Illus. 1-10. *A close look at the features of the Delta 18-inch C-arm saw. This saw has a variable-speed control providing speeds of 40 to 2,000 spm.*

Illus. 1-11 (below). *Some of the major parts of the RBI Hawk 20-inch floor model, shown with the worktable removed for clarity. Note the arm's pivot points.*

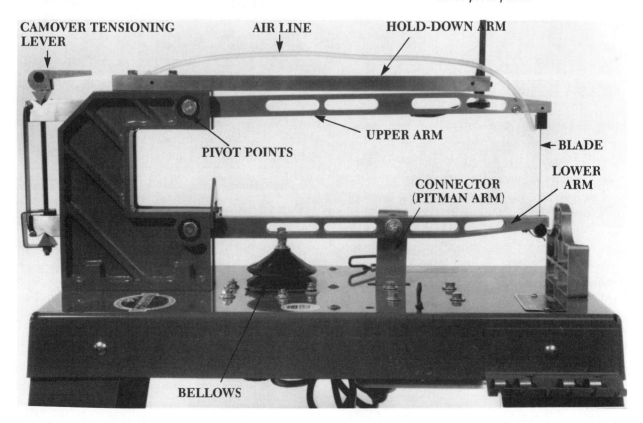

CAMOVER TENSIONING LEVER

AIR LINE

HOLD-DOWN ARM

UPPER ARM

PIVOT POINTS

BLADE

LOWER ARM

CONNECTOR (PITMAN ARM)

BELLOWS

Illus. 1-12. *The principal parts from an RBI scroll saw that convert rotary motion from the motor into the up-and-down reciprocating movement. The connector, also called the pitman arm, is linked to the lower arm of the saw.*

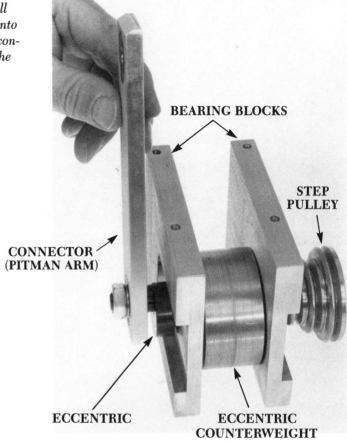

Motors and Speed-Changing Devices

The motors that power modern scroll saws are usually ⅟₁₀ or ⅛ horsepower; some are ¼ horsepower. Motors are linked to the lower arms to drive the saw up and down in one of four different ways. One way is a direct-link *single-speed* (usually around 1,725 spm) motor. (See Illus. 1-13.) The second type has the same direct-drive linkage, but the motor is controlled by a *two-speed* selector switch. Its highest speeds are approximately 1,725-1,800 spm, and its slowest speeds are approximately 860-900 spm. (See Illus. 1-14–1-16.)

The *belted-drive* system is another way power from the motor is made to move the saw. This system of step pulleys provides a range of two (slow or fast), three, or four selected, fixed speeds. (See Illus. 1-12 and 1-17.)

The final and most convenient speed-controlling system is the *variable-speed-control* mechanism. (See Illus. 1-18–1-21.) As the term indicates, the motor in this system can be adjusted to different rates of speed.

Air Blowers

Air blowers help remove sawdust from the cutting path so that the operator can see and follow the layout lines. Most saws generate their own air supply from an air-pumping bellows located under the lower arm; the air is fed to the cutting area via a plastic hose. On some saws, the air supply is adequate, and on others it is inadequate. Some saws simply do not have any supply. There is not one commercially produced air-blower system available today that does not have disadvantages.

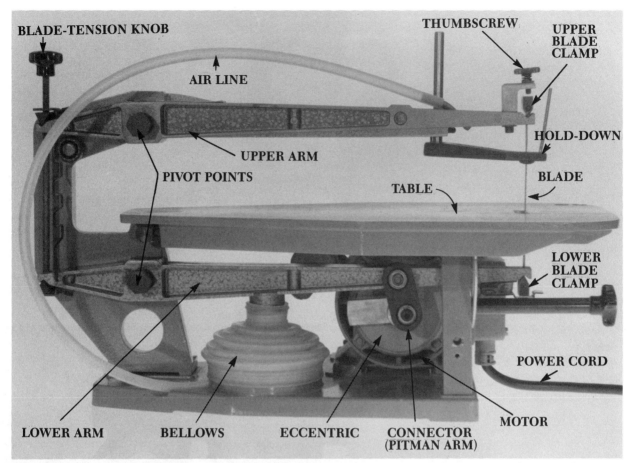

Illus. 1-13. *This view of a Hegner single-speed saw shows the connector (pitman arm) linked from the motor eccentric directly to the lower arm.*

Air blowers are further explored in Chapter 3 (page 41).

Guards and Hold-downs

Guards and hold-downs are safety devices that can be found on all scroll saws. (See Illus. 1-22–1-24.) A hold-down is used to keep the material flat on the table and prevent it from moving up and down. A guard prevents the scroll-sawyer from coming into contact with the blade.

Though guards and hold-downs are often more troublesome than they are useful, beginners should continue to use them until they are totally familiar with and are able to control the cutting action of the saw. When you reach this point,

simply remove the hold-down, the hold-down arm, and the guard in those cutting situations where they interfere with the sawing.

Blade-Tension Controls

Blade-tension controls come in several basic styles. A rear screw is the most common type of blade-tension control. (See Illus. 1-5 and 1-13.) Another type, a rear cam lever that can only be found on RBI Hawk saws, works quickly once it is adjusted. (See Illus. 1-11.) A third type of tensioning mechanism that is appearing on more and more scroll saws is located up front, rather than reaching all the way to the rear.

Illus. 1-14. *Dremel's two-speed 16-inch saw takes either plain- or pin-end blades. (See Chapter 2.) Note the blade-changing clamp fixture on the upper arm cover.*

Illus. 1-15. *A close look at the two-speed selector switch on the Dremel 16-inch scroll saw. Note the table-tilt system at the left.*

Illus. 1-16. *Delta sells a 16-inch two-speed, parallel-arm, bench-top saw.*

Illus. 1-17. *The blade speed in strokes per minute on the Sakura Scroll Mate is changed by positioning this small, stretchable drive belt on the appropriate step of the pulley.*

Illus. 1-18. *The Sears 16-inch variable-speed scroll saw adjusts from 500 to 1,500 spm.*

Illus. 1-19. *A close-up look at the variable-speed on/off control switch on the Sears 16-inch scroll saw.*

Illus. 1-20. *Hegner's 18-inch variable-speed saw has a 2⅝-inch-stock thickness-cutting capacity.*

Illus. 1-21. *A closer look at Hegner's 18-inch variable-speed saw, showing its on/off speed control and table-tilting features.*

Illus. 1-22. *This device, which is found on many of the lower-priced saws, serves only as a guard, and is totally ineffective as a hold-down.*

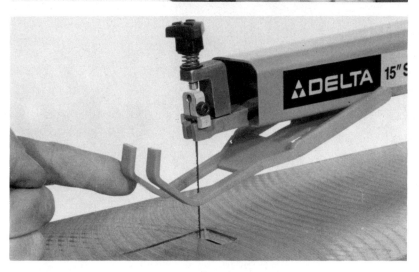

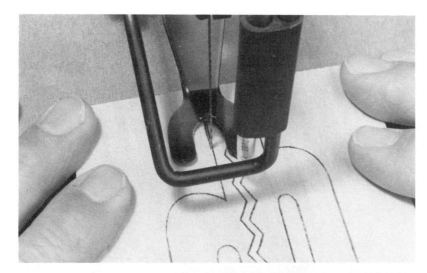

Illus. 1-23. *Some hold-downs, guards, and blowers are time-consuming to adjust, have marginal performance qualities, and sometimes visually obstruct the operator's view of the cutting path in front of the blade.*

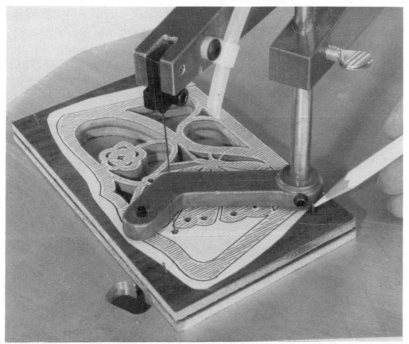

Illus. 1-24. *Sometimes, regardless of how well a hold-down is designed and functions, it is not effective when openings cut into the workpiece pass under it. It may also get in the way during certain jobs such as the one shown here, where a nail holding two pieces together (for identical cutting) strikes the hold-down, inhibiting the feed.*

Blade-Suspension Systems

The blade-suspension system consists of the devices which clamp to the blade ends (blade clamps) and the provisions at the ends of the arms that permit the blade clamps to pivot or rock during operation. The design and performance of the blade clamps and the way they move or work on the arms is extremely important. This is the single most important design element that affects overall saw performance. Most scroll-sawing frustrations originate from faulty blade clamps.

There are many different types of blade clamps and blade-suspension systems that vary greatly from manufacturer to manufacturer. In an effort to acquaint the reader with all the choices—and there are many—we will take a close look at the most popular types and brands.

The most basic suspension system is that designed to incorporate pin-end scroll-saw blades.

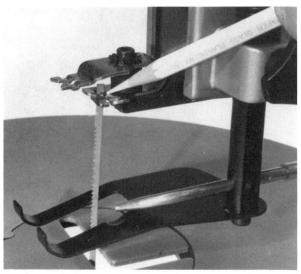

Illus. 1-25. *Note how a pin-end blade fits into the holder on the end of the arm of a Sears saw. This holder permits installing the blade in any of four positions, with the teeth facing forward, to the right, as shown here, to the left, or to the rear.*

Illus. 1-26. *This Dremel blade holder is similar to the one on the Sears saw. It too will take pin-end blades, and also has a provision for receiving a pivoting blade clamp for plain-end blades. See Illus. 1-27 and 1-28.*

Illus. 1-27. *The Dremel blade clamp for plain-end blades.*

(See Chapter 2.) A shallow V-like depression on the arm saddles the pin, which is part of the blade. (See Illus. 1-25 and 1-26.) Some Sears, Dremel, and a few imported saws are designed to carry either pin-end blades or the more preferred plain-end blades (blades without pins). Pin-end blades are considerably larger (wider, not necessarily longer) than plain-end blades and eventually become impractical to use because they cannot make fine, detailed cuts that require sharp turns.

Manufacturers are slowly realizing the importance of providing quick-changing and easy-to-use blade-suspension systems for use with small, narrower plain-end blades, but most manufac-turers have yet to incorporate one in their saws. Too many blade clamps require the use of an allen wrench. (See Illus. 1-27.) Some blade clamps, like those used on Dremel's scroll saws, hang and swing from the arms. (See Illus. 1-27 and 1-28.)

Most of the inexpensive Taiwanese or Asian imported saws have poor-quality blade clamps. These clamps, shown in Illus. 1-29 and 1-30, are found on almost all of the low-priced saws. They are difficult to use in that they are awkward to hold while tightening the little allen screws that are usually made of soft metal. These clamps have very little gripping area to secure the blade.

This style of blade clamp and blade suspension

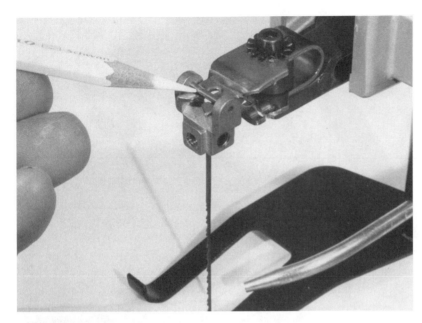

Illus. 1-28. *The Dremel blade clamp hangs and pivots on the blade holder of the arm.*

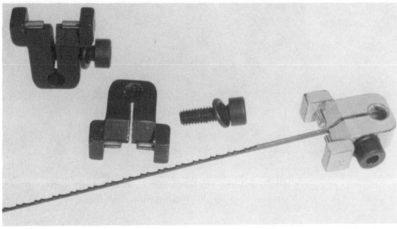

Illus. 1-29. *This blade-clamp design is found on almost all of the lower-priced Taiwanese saws.*

system is often standard equipment on many saws and is without question the major cause of user disappointment and frustration. Later, we will explore some ways to reduce a few of the problems associated with the use of this particular style of blade clamp.

Parallel flat-jaw blade clamps come in different configurations. (See Illus. 1-31–1-34.) On some saws, this type of blade clamp is easier to use than on others. Flat-jaw blade clamps often require special blade-changing fixtures that hold the clamp and/or blade as it is tightened with an allen wrench or special tool.

The American-made RBI saw has an unusual but efficient cylindrical lower blade clamp that slips into a bronze bearing. (See Illus. 1-34 and 1-35.)

The German-made Hegner scroll saw has blade-suspension features that distinguish it from other scroll saws. Its knife-edge blade-suspension design features minimal pivotal friction, and the key-style wrench included is fairly easy to use. (See Illus. 1-36 and 1-37.)

Seyco Sales Co., of Garland, Texas sells a blade clamp with which you can change blades very quickly. This blade clamp is available as an accessory that can be purchased to fit most major brands of scroll saw. (See Illus. 1-38 and 1-39.)

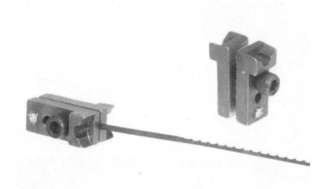

Illus. 1-31. *The parallel flat-jaw blade clamp on the Heartwood scroll saw.*

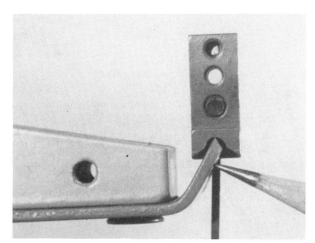

Illus. 1-32. *Here's how the blade clamp pivots on the upper arm of the Heartwood scroll saw.*

Illus. 1-30. *The Taiwanese blade holder, as it fits into the v-notch on the end of the arm.*

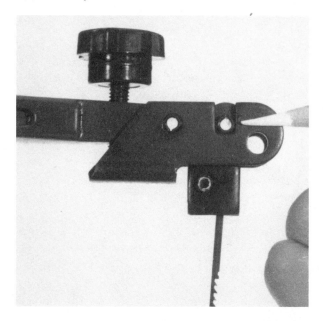

Illus. 1-33. *The parallel flat-jaw blade clamp on this Sears saw hangs and pivots on the hollow pin indicated by the pencil.*

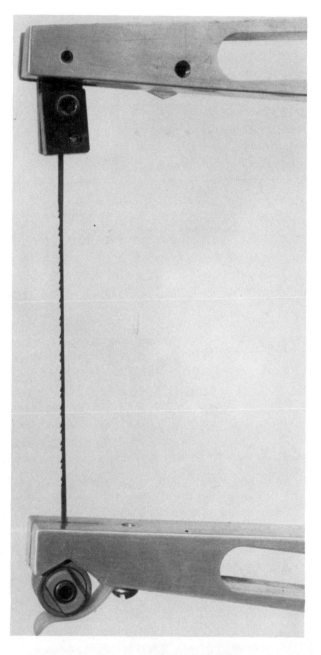

Illus. 1-34. *The blade-suspension system on the RBI Hawk combines two different blade clamps—a parallel flat-jaw clamp (above) and a cylindrical blade clamp that fits into a bronze bearing (below).*

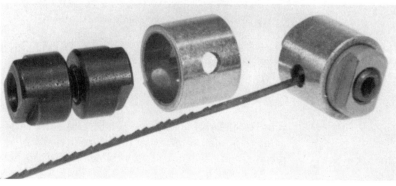

Illus. 1-35. *A closer look at the components of the lower-blade clamp. The outer, oil-impregnated bronze-bearing shell reduces pivotal friction.*

Illus. 1-36. *The blade clamp and key-style wrench used on a Hegner saw.*

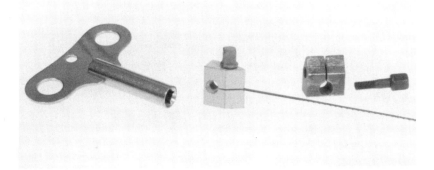

Illus. 1-37. *The blade clamp on the Hegner saw can pivot easily.*

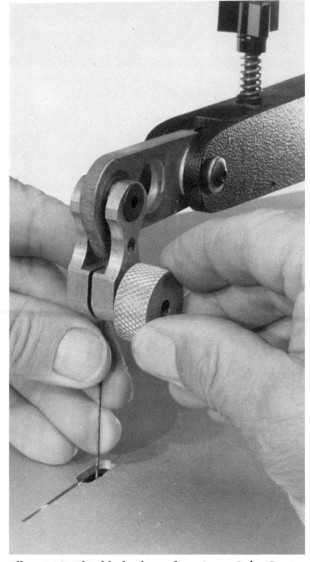

Illus. 1-38. *This blade clamp from Seyco Sales Co. is made to fit almost all saws. It features a quick blade release, and the operator can tighten it with his fingers, as shown.*

Illus. 1-39. *A closer look at Seyco's blade clamp, made for the larger Excalibur scroll saw. Seyco makes similar clamps that fit on most other saws.*

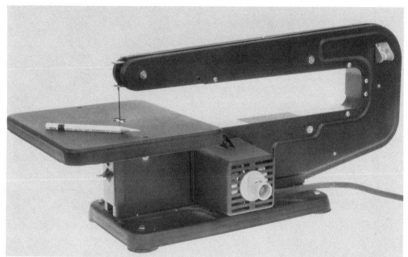

Illus. 1-40. *The Dremel light-duty scroll saw has a 15-inch throat capacity, carries only 3-inch pin-end blades, and is best suited for cutting thinner material.*

Illus. 1-41. *This Sears 16-inch parallel-arm saw carries only 5-inch pin-end blades and cuts hardwoods up to 1 inch thick. It is not intended for fine-detail sawing.*

Determining Which Scroll Saw to Buy

There are approximately 50 different models or brands of scroll saw available today. Most manufacturers are represented in one or more of the illustrations in this chapter. Some of the low-priced Asian imports have the very same design and manufacturer as other scroll saws, but just carry a different brand or label. (See Illus. 1-42–1-44.)

It is not easy to determine which scroll saw to buy. Such an evaluation depends on several factors: your present and future gross-sawing needs, what you expect from the saw, and how much you are capable of paying.

Because the cost of a saw plays such an important part in the selection process, it is important that you be given an overview of the types of scroll saw available in certain price ranges. But before this is explored, you should be aware of the following point: An expensive scroll saw is not necessarily a high-quality, productive scroll saw. Effective and non-effective scroll saws can be found in almost any price category.

There are two saws available that are priced under $100. These are the light-duty Dremel and Sears saws which carry only pin-end blades, and which cut softwoods best.

There are many more scroll saws available in the $200-$300 price range. Most of the saws that fall in this category are imports, and they can sometimes be inconvenient and frustrating to use. You'll have to tolerate such things as more-difficult-to-use blade clamps, blades that break more frequently, parts made with soft metals where they should be hard, etc. After a certain amount of use, major parts will wear. Bearings may need replacement, threads will strip, and allen wrench sockets will become rounded. On occasion, the arms may break from fatigue. However, the occasional scroll-saw user and non-professional can upgrade some of the cheaper import saws to some extent. Turn to Chapter 3 for more information.

Not all imported saws are of poor quality. Two popular professional-quality saws—the Excalibur 24-inch saw and the Hegner 19½-inch Polymax saw—come, respectively, from Canada and Germany. Saws of this high quality set the standards by which others are measured. They are also much more expensive than poorer-quality imported saws.

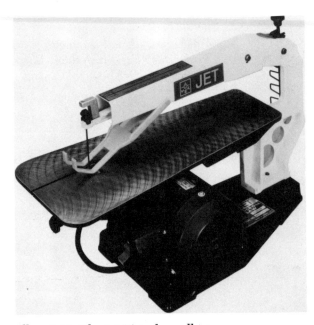

Illus. 1-42. *The Jet 15-inch scroll saw.*

Illus. 1-43. *The Delta 15-inch scroll saw is also imported from Taiwan.*

Bench saws are less expensive then similar floor models, and most bench saws can be mounted on optional stands at any time. (See Illus. 1-42–1-46.)

One saw that has some unusual design innovations is the Fretmaster. (See Illus. 1-47.) This economically priced saw is manufactured by Reidle Products, Box 661, Richland Center, Wisconsin 53581. It is specifically intended for fretwork (a type of scroll-sawing that involves many inside cuts). The saw features a sit-down operating height, an 18-inch throat, one of the quickest, non-complicated blade-changing systems available, and a healthy 1¼-inch cutting stroke. However, its maximum speed is only 575 spm, which is ideal for highly detailed work in thin stock, but too slow for cutting thick material. Thus, the saw is best suited for sawing material ¾-inch and less in thickness.

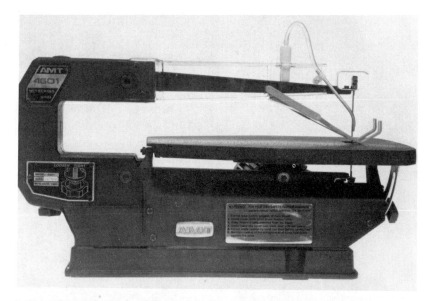

Illus. 1-44. *This AMT 16-inch bench saw takes both 5-inch pin- and plain-end blades.*

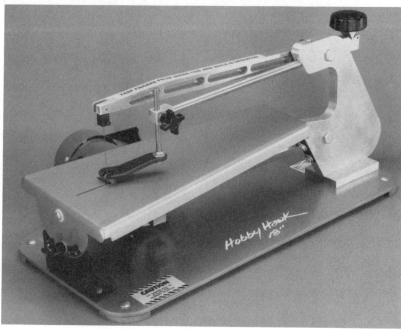

Illus. 1-45. *This 18-inch bench saw, called the Hobby Hawk, is the latest scroll saw from RBI. Less expensive than other RBI Hawk saws, it has some of the same features.*

Illus. 1-46. *The newest scroll saw from Hegner is the economy-model hobby saw, Multimax 14E. This bench-top unit has many of the same features as Hegner's more expensive floor models.*

Illus. 1-47. *The Fretmaster saw, manufactured by Reidle Products, has two special features: a sit-down operating height that is very comfortable, and one of the quickest blade-installation systems. It is designed to cut softwood up to ¾ inch thick. It has an 18-inch throat, a 1¼-inch stroke, and cuts at the rate of 575 spm.*

Selecting a Saw

Do not rush into buying a saw. Instead, try as many different saws as possible. Use a friend's saw or try to use different saws at your local tool dealer's store or at your local school shop. The saw you select should be of the proper size and weight to meet your sawing needs, and should be one you can afford. Also, make sure that the manufacturer can replace or repair the parts. Be aware that imported saws have metric threads.

Before selecting a specific saw, make sure that it has the following features:

1. Quietness of operation.

2. Freedom from vibration.

3. High-quality bearings.

4. Good electrical features (motors and switches).

Illus. 1-48. *With the power off, check both arms for side-to-side movement, which indicates poor alignment, bad or cheap bearings, or improper assembly. This condition will lead to eventual parts replacement and immediately contribute to a high frequency of blade breakage.*

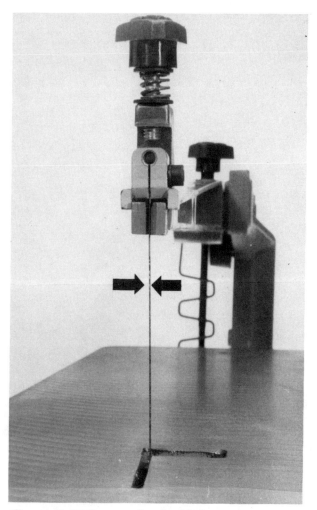

Illus. 1-49. *Make sure that the blade on your saw does not wobble when you turn the saw on. You can detect blade wobble by looking at the blade from the operator's position. The blade will appear to be a blur.*

5. Springs which immediately lift the upper arm when a blade breaks. This is an important safety feature.

6. High-quality blade clamps that are easy to use and permit quick-blade installation.

7. A good hold-down—one that can swing out of the way when not being used, without you having to remove the blade.

8. A blade-tensioning control that is easy to use and adjust.

9. Few parts that require an allen wrench.

10. No side play in the arms. Side play can be detected as a visual blur of the blade during operation. This situation causes blade friction when it rubs on the sides of the cut, and leads to frequent, frustrating blade breakage. (See Illus. 1-48 and 1-49.)

11. A two-speed or variable-speed saw, if you're going to cut a wide variety of materials, thick or thin and in varying degrees of complexity.

Chapter 2

SCROLL-SAW BLADES

The novice will marvel at the very thin, narrow blades that can be used on constant-tension scroll saws without breaking. Scroll-saw blades are inexpensive. They range in price from 15 to 75 cents, depending on the supplier, the quality of the blades, and how many blades you are buying.

When selecting the one optimum blade for a particular cutting situation, there are several factors to consider: the actual species or kind of wood material being cut; the cutting speed (spm) of the saw; the complexity of the curve or pattern detail required; and the surface finish of the cut desired. Because of the many factors involved, it is far more useful to provide the beginner with information describing the types and sizes of blade available, and the pertinent guidelines for selecting blades. This is given below.

Types of Blade

There are two distinct types of scroll-saw blade: pin-end blades and 5-inch plain-end (pinless) blades. (See Illus. 2-1 and 2-2.) Plain-end blades come in a greater variety of sizes and offer greater

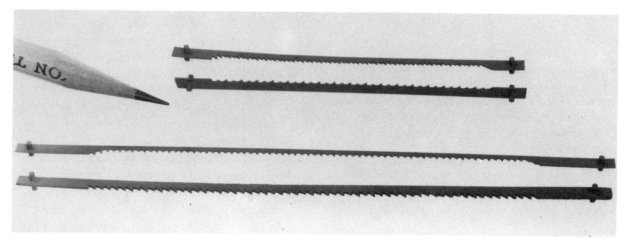

Illus. 2-1. *Pin-end blades come in two lengths: 3 inches (top), for the Dremel light-duty saw, and 5 inches (below), for Sears, Dremel, and some impor-* *ted saws. Each length of blade comes in two types: fine (third blade from top) and coarse (bottom).*

Illus. 2-2. *Comparing a 5-inch pin-end blade (left) to a 5-inch plain-end blade. Note that a larger hole has to be made for the pin-end blade (for the pin) so that it can saw out inside openings. This makes it more difficult to use a pin-end blade to make highly detailed, ornate cuts.*

sawing versatility; consequently, they are more popular.

Plain-end blades can be sub-categorized as follows: (1) scroll blades, (2) fret blades, and (3) spiral blades. (See Illus. 2-3.) There is actually a fourth

type of plain-end blade—metal-piercing or jewelers blades—but since these are not wood-cutting blades, they will not be examined here. The other types of plain-end blade are explored below.

Scroll Blades

Scroll blades are coarse-cutting blades. They have regular-style standard saw teeth similar to those on a handsaw. These blades are best suited for cutting thick or hard materials that cannot be cut effectively with other blades. Most pin-end blades are scroll blades.

Fret Blades

Fret blades are preferred by scroll-sawyers. They are much narrower than scroll blades, and can be used to cut very fine or intricate details, when necessary. They have a skip-tooth design. The space provided by the skip-tooth design provides more room for sawdust to be carried out of the cut. This means that the blade will cut cooler because there is less friction in the cut (kerf). Ultimately, this will result in less blade breakage. A double-tooth skip fret-blade design is fairly new and seems to be gaining popularity among professionals.

Spiral Blades

Spiral blades are simply regular blades twisted so that their teeth point outward in different directions. (See Illus. 2-3.) They are available in fine-to-medium sizes. You can use spiral blades to saw in all directions without turning the workpiece, and can make sharp, zero-radius cuts, to name just two advantages. However, spiral blades are not recommended for the first-time scroll sawyer because they cut a wider-than-normal kerf (sawing path) and require more skill in maneuvering the workpiece.

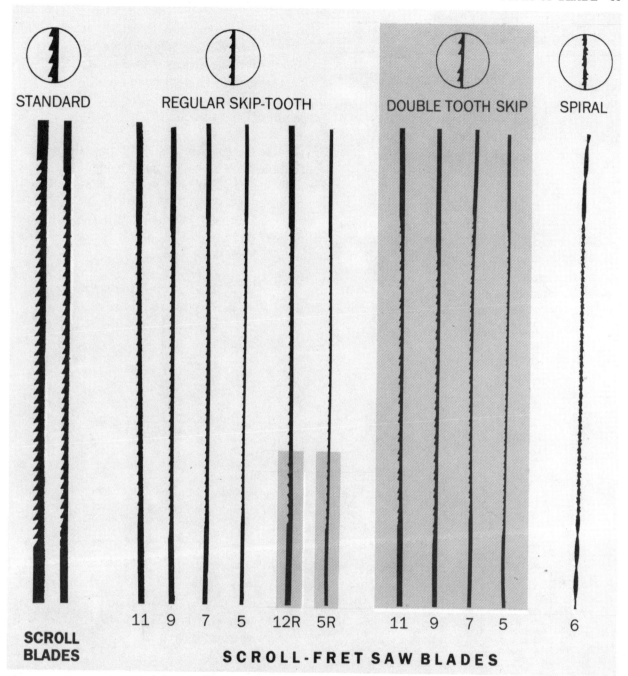

STANDARD

REGULAR SKIP-TOOTH

DOUBLE TOOTH SKIP

SPIRAL

11   9   7   5   12R   5R   11   9   7   5   6

SCROLL BLADES

SCROLL-FRET SAW BLADES

Illus. 2-3. *The most popular or widely used blades, shown full size. Those most highly recommended for handling almost all beginning sawing jobs are in the grey-shaded areas.*

Blade Sizes

Technically, the size of the saw blade is determined by the blade's width, thickness, the number of teeth per inch, its length, and the type of tooth profile. Almost all fret blades are classified according to a generic numbering system that ranges from 0 to 12. The larger the blade's number, the larger the blade.

A beginner will find himself using No. 5, 7, 9, and 11 blades for most of his work. Blades in this size category will handle 95% of all scroll-sawing jobs, whether the wood material used is thick, thin, hard, or soft.

Thick hardwoods are generally best cut with coarser (fewer teeth per inch), larger blades. Softwoods of thin to medium thickness (½ to 1 inch) can be cut very effectively with a wide variety of different types and sizes of blades.

Following are guidelines and information that will help you determine which size blade to use in specific cutting situations:

1. Use the coarsest blade that gives the quality of cut needed. Larger (coarser) blades have fewer teeth than small blades, and, consequently, are tougher and less likely to break under the same sawing conditions. Therefore, it makes sense to first select a coarse blade and then work towards the finer blades.

2. Use a No. 12, 11, or 9 blade for general cutting of thick hardwoods and softwoods.

Universal Generic No.	TPI (Teeth Per Inch)	Material Cut/Usage
2/0	28	For extremely intricate sawing and very thin cuts in ⅟₁₆″ to ³⁄₃₂″ material. Excellent for cutting wood veneer, plastic, hard rubber, pearl, etc.
0	25	
1	23	
2	20	For tight radius work in thin materials ³⁄₃₂″ to ⅛″, wood veneer, wood, bone, fibre, ivory, plastic, etc.
3	18	
4	15	
5	14	For close radius-cutting in material ⅛″ or thicker. Great for sawing hard/softwood, bone, horn, plastic, etc.
6	13	
7	12	Popular sizes for cutting hard and soft woods ³⁄₁₆″ up to 2″. Also cut plastic, paper, felt, bone, etc.
8	11.5	
9	11.5	
10	11	
11	9.5	
12	9.5	

Table 1. *Blade sizes, and their suggested uses. The term TPI indicates the number of teeth per inch.*

3. Use a No. 9 or 7 blade for cutting moderate details in hard or soft woods ½ inch to 1½ inches thick.

4. Use a No. 5 blade to cut fine details in materials that range in thickness from thin (⅛ inch) to medium (1 inch).

5. It's almost impossible to visually distinguish any difference in the surface quality or smoothness of a cut made with a No. 5 or 9 blade. Both make extremely smooth cuts.

6. Make sure that you don't use a blade that is too coarse (has too few teeth) when sawing thin material. (See Illus. 2-4.)

Some of the very best blades may tear or leave feathering along the cut where the blade exits out of the bottom surface. (See Illus. 2-5.) One option available to minimize tearing or feathering on the bottom of the workpiece is to use a reverse-tooth blade design. The blades labelled 12R and 5R in Illus. 2-3 have a reverse-tooth design. The R designates blades that have their lower teeth reversed. The No. 5R blade is recommended for cutting detail in materials of thinner to medium thickness.

Almost all scroll blades are made with a slight burr or ragged edge along one side of the blade. (See Illus. 2-6.) The sharp burr edge is the result

Illus. 2-4. *When sawing thin materials, be sure that at least two, preferably three, teeth will be in contact with the material at all times. Here, for example, a No. 9 blade with 12 teeth per inch can be used to saw this ¼-inch-thick material.*

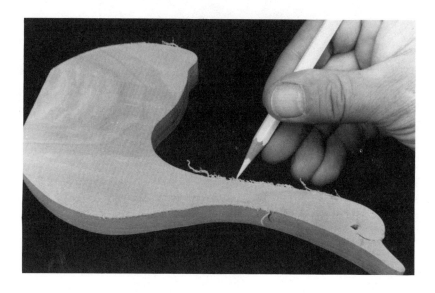

Illus. 2-5. *This condition, which is known as feathering, occurs on the blade's exit side (bottom) of the workpiece. This common, but not serious, condition can be minimized when you use blades that have their lower teeth reversed.*

of material flow of the metal as the blade is milled or stamped out while it is being manufactured. The burr-edge side is sharper and provides less cutting resistance than the non-burr side of the blade, but it also makes a slightly rougher cut surface. This causes the blade to track slightly to one side during the cut. This condition is actually very slight, and is so quickly compensated for by the scroll-sawyer that it is of very little consequence. However, it is important to be aware of this condition, especially when sawing in a straight line. Refer to page 85.

Burr edges can be removed from the back and sides of the blade. This, in some cases, increases the blade's cutting performance. To remove the burr, carefully place a fine stone hone against the side of the moving blade. (See Illus 2-7.) Be careful not to bring the file or hone too far around, working it on the front of the teeth. This would seriously inhibit their cutting action.

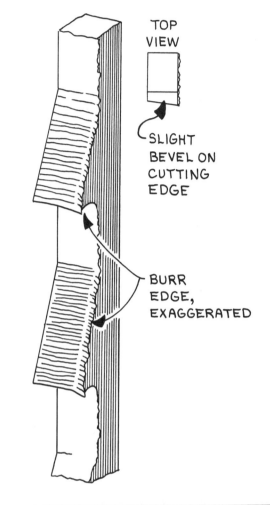

Illus. 2-6. This enlarged sketch shows the sharp microscopic metal burr along one edge of the blade. This condition is typical of almost all scroll-saw blades. It is caused by the way blades are manufactured. For this reason, scroll-saw blades actually track unevenly because there is more cutting resistance on one edge of the blade than the other.

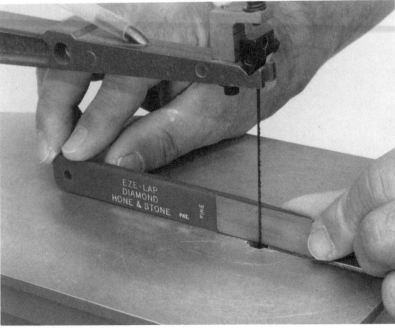

Illus. 2-7. Carefully honing the burr side of the blade, as shown, will help it make smoother cuts in some materials such as certain plastics.

It is a good idea to round and remove the sharp corners at the rear of the blade. (See Illus. 2-8 and 2-9.) This technique permits sharper turns and minimizes friction in the cut. This is especially useful when you want to improve the radius-cutting capabilities of the typically wider pin-end blades. (See Illus 2-10.)

You can further modify pin-end blades so that you can make piercing cuts and inside cuts to produce fine detail work. More information on this is provided in Chapter 9.

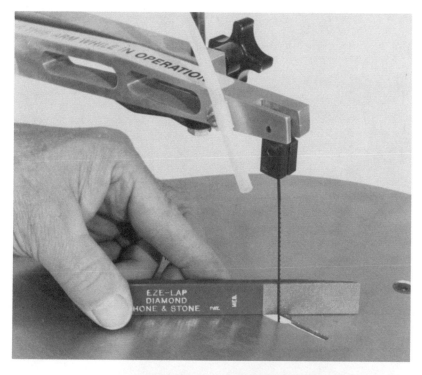

Illus. 2-8. Rounding the sharp, back edges, as shown, allows the blade to make sharper turns and minimizes frictional heat.

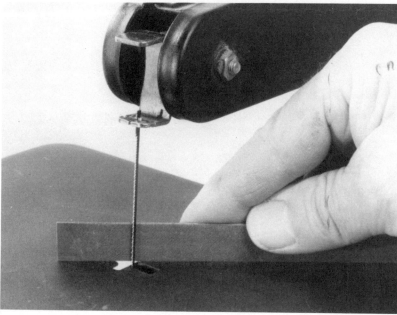

Illus. 2-9. Rounding the rear corners of a pin-end blade on a Dremel saw with a fine, single-cut file.

Illus. 2-10. *This sharper-than-usual radius cut was made in ¾-inch-thick oak on a Sears saw with a pin-end blade with rounded rear edges.*

Chapter 3

UPGRADING IMPORTED SAWS

As discussed in Chapter 1, there are affordably priced 15-inch Asian saws on the market that are apparently made by the same Taiwan manufacturer. (See Illus. 3-1.) They appear under the following manufacturers' names: Rexon, Penn, State, Grizzley, Jet, Nu-Mark, Value Craft, Total Shop, AMT, Delta, Powermatic, Sunhill, Super Scroll (18 inch), and other names. They seem to be modelled after the first Hegner saws. These Asian saws can be modified to function better. An upgraded saw will not perform as well as a $500-$700 production saw, but it will prove to be a good hobby saw. An upgraded saw should eliminate or reduce many of the frustrations associated with the cheaper saws if used as they are from the factory.

Some of the problems associated with imported scroll saws are as follow:

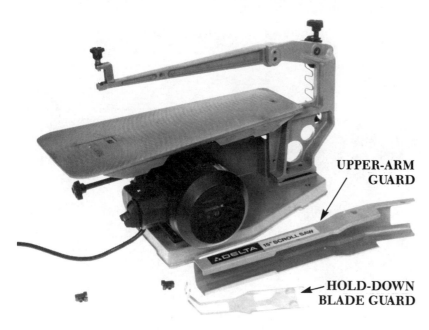

UPPER-ARM GUARD

HOLD-DOWN BLADE GUARD

Illus. 3-1. *This Delta 15-inch saw is typical of the many Asian imports that are so similar.*

1. Rough table surfaces

2. No, or an ineffective, sawdust blower.

3. A table slot that does not extend fully out to the edge.

4. Poor-quality blade clamps that have soft-metal screws.

5. No blade-changing fixture.

6. No floor stand.

7. An ineffective hold-down.

Most of these problems can be easily and cheaply corrected. Also, be aware that there are accessories and attachments that can be used to improve the performance of imported scroll saws.

Begin modifying your saw by smoothing the rough surfaces of the milled cast-iron worktable. Use 180- or 220-grit wet/dry abrasive under a hardwood block with light oil as a lubricant. (See Illus. 3-2.) Polish the surface, working towards smoother 360- or 400-grit abrasives. Clean the surface with mineral spirits, and then dry and apply a paste wax. (See Illus. 3-3.) Wax will prevent rusting and make it easier to feed stock on the saw. Waxing the table is a good idea for any saw.

Illus. 3-2. *Smooth the cast-iron table first with 180–400 grit wet/dry abrasive, and then change gradually to finer-grit abrasives (360 or 400 grit).*

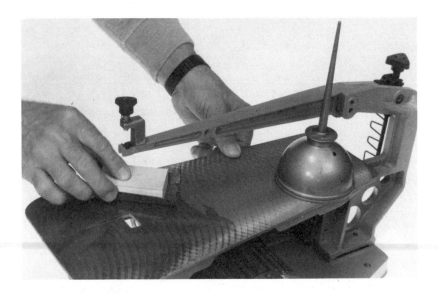

Illus. 3-3. *Clean the oil away with mineral spirits, and then dry and polish the surface with thin coat(s) of hard paste wax.*

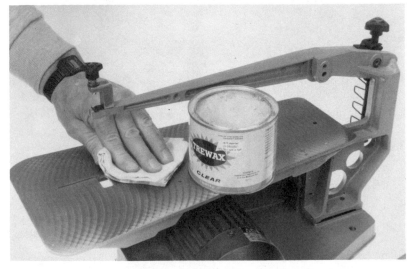

Illus. 3-4. *A small aquarium pump supplies the air for the sawdust blower on this 15-inch imported scroll saw.*

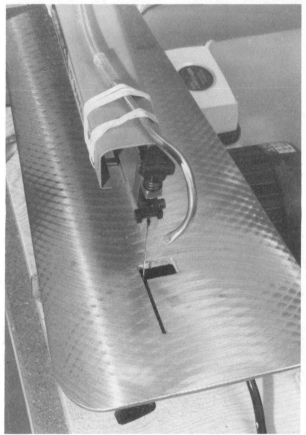

Illus. 3-5. *The air from the aquarium pump is fed into this copper tubing nozzle. Note how the copper is slightly flattened at the end and bent to deflect sawdust away from the operator. Several rubber bands stretched over the tubing hold it all in place.*

There are several ways to deal with the lack of or a poorly performing sawdust blower. Sawdust blower attachment kits are available from Advanced Machinery Imports, New Castle, Delaware and Penn State Industries, Philadelphia, Pennsylvania. Another solution is a small aquarium pump, available locally or by mail from Highland Hardware, Atlanta, Georgia, to propel air to the cutting area via plastic and copper tubing. (See Illus. 3-4 and 3-5.)

If you have an air supply (compressor) in your shop, you can set up an excellent sawdust blower. (See Illus. 3-6.) Simply connect a flow-control valve with female threads (in and out) and adjustable plastic coolant hose (Illus. 3-7) of the type used in metal machining to the air supply hose. These parts can be purchased from industrial supply companies specializing in metal work tooling.

Cutting a full length, to-the-edge, table slot is another modification worth considering. A full slot will make it easier and quicker to change blades. (See Illus. 3-8–3-10.) However, be aware that when you saw a slot from the edge to match up with the existing slot there is a possibility you could release stresses in the table casting which could cause it to become warped or uneven. This may be a chance that is worth taking. And if your table should warp, it can be fitted or overlaid with a good auxiliary table, one you can make yourself. (See page 95.)

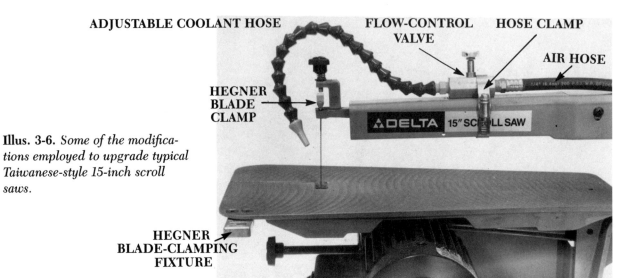

ADJUSTABLE COOLANT HOSE   **FLOW-CONTROL VALVE**   **HOSE CLAMP**   **AIR HOSE**

HEGNER BLADE CLAMP

HEGNER BLADE-CLAMPING FIXTURE

Illus. 3-6. *Some of the modifications employed to upgrade typical Taiwanese-style 15-inch scroll saws.*

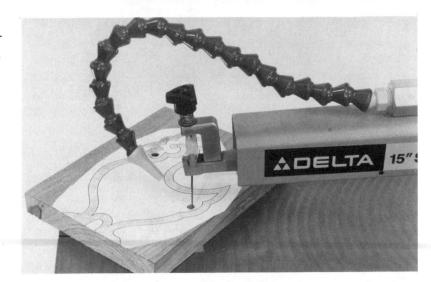

Illus. 3-7. *This adjustable coolant hose, which has an inside diameter of ¼ inch, can be easily positioned, without springing back, to direct air and dust away from the operator, as shown. This system is much safer and healthier than almost any other dust-blower system which directs the air flow towards the operator. (See Illus. 5-2 and 5-3.)*

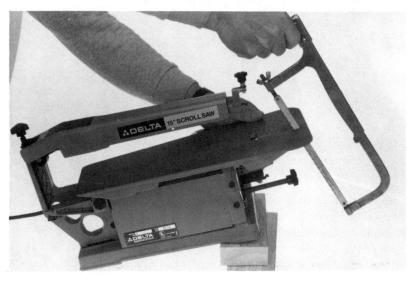

Illus. 3-8. *Cutting the cast-iron table with a hacksaw to make a slot that extends all the way to the edge will speed up blade changes.*

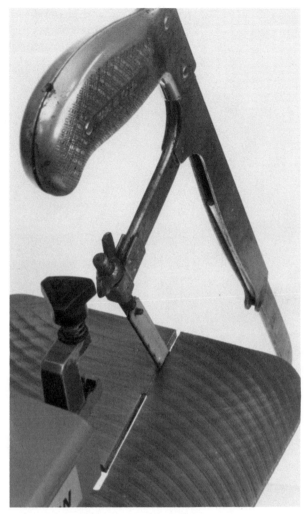

Illus. 3-9. *A close-up look at the cutting process. Three hacksaw blades mounted in the hacksaw frame cut the slot to its desired width. The soft cast iron can be cut easily.*

The almost unsuitable blade clamps that come with imported saws will be much easier to use if you make a simple blade-clamping fixture designed to hold the blade clamp as its screw is tightened with the allen wrench. This fixture is simply a sawn-out or chiselled pocket cut into a small piece of wood that cradles the blade clamp. It is then mounted to the workbench or to the corner of an auxiliary wood base. (See Illus. 3-11–3-13.)

The same wooden blade-clamping fixture can be used for Hegner blade clamps if you decide to use this manufacturer's blade-clamping system, which is considerably better. (See Illus. 3-14–3-16.) You may want to purchase Hegner's complete "up grade" kit, which includes blade clamps, a table-mounted blade-changing fixture, and an easy-to-use key-style wrench that tightens the hardened square-headed screws on the blade clamps. (See Illus. 3-17–3-19.) Hegner scroll saw parts can be obtained from Advanced Machinery Imports Ltd., New Castle, Delaware.

As previously mentioned, inexpensive saw stands such as the ones shown in Illus. 1-9 are available if you would prefer a freestanding floor model saw. And if you should determine that a better hold-down is necessary, contact Highland Hardware in Atlanta, Georgia for a copy of their Delta saw owner's manual supplement, which gives plans/patterns for making a good hold-down, along with other helpful information on getting the maximum out of the Taiwanese-made Delta 15-inch scroll saw.

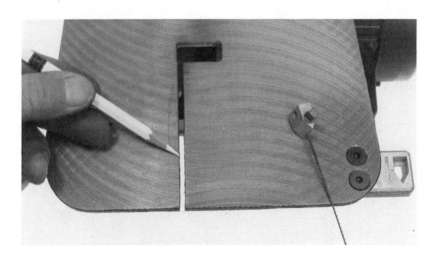

Illus. 3-10. *The extended blade slot as cut entirely to the edge. Soften the sharp edges with a file or abrasive and a wood block. Note the Hegner blade-clamping fixture mounted on the right.*

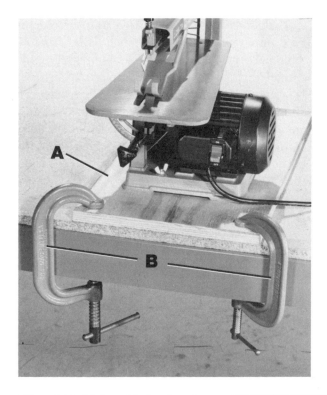

Illus. 3-11. *Make sure that the saw is fastened down securely before using it. To maintain portability or conserve bench space, it may be to your advantage to mount the saw to a wood base (A), which, in turn, can be clamped (B) to a worktable or bench when needed. Foam or rubber washers placed under the saw may help reduce excessive vibration.*

Illus. 3-12. *Make a blade-changing pocket fixture and mount it to the auxiliary base or to a workbench. To make the fixture, cut an opening through a hardwood block that's sized to cradle the blade clamp, as shown in Illus. 3-13.*

Illus. 3-13. *The homemade blade-clamp pocket fixture makes it easier to use the imported blade clamp. This simple device holds the blade clamp steady as you insert the blade into the clamp and tighten it with an allen wrench, as shown.*

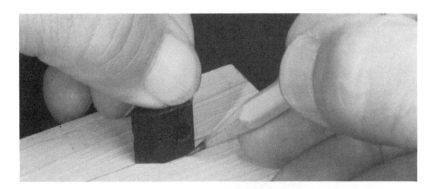

Illus. 3-14. *Trace around the slotted Hegner blade clamp. Carefully cut out the "pocket," sawing to the line to make a very close fit.*

Illus. 3-15. *Blade clamp "pockets" should be of the appropriate depth, so that when a blade is placed on the wood surface it will slide directly into the slotted opening of the blade clamp.*

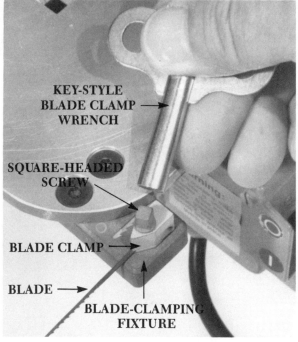

KEY-STYLE BLADE CLAMP WRENCH

SQUARE-HEADED SCREW

BLADE CLAMP

BLADE

BLADE-CLAMPING FIXTURE

Illus. 3-17. *Hegner's upgrade kit includes the same blade clamps, a table-mounted blade-changing fixture, and a key-style wrench that come as standard equipment with the more expensive Hegner saws.*

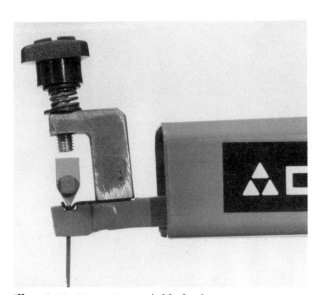

Illus. 3-16. *Using Hegner's blade clamps on an imported saw.*

Illus. 3-18. *Mounting the Hegner blade-clamping fixture block to the saw table of the imported saw. Mark the center-to-center holes carefully and drill small pilot holes. The center-to-center holes must line up with the center-to-center distance of the holes on the Hegner blade-clamping fixture block.*

Illus. 3-19. *After the holes are drilled, countersink the screw heads so that they are flush or slightly below the table surface.*

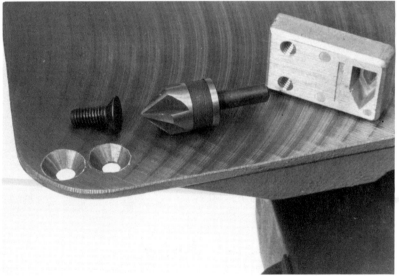

Chapter 4

WOOD MATERIAL

The effective scroll sawyer—and woodworkers in general—must be able to choose the wood or wood material that has the properties best suited for a particular project. Effective woodworkers can only make such a judgment if they are aware of the basic characteristics of the different types of wood and wood material available. This information is given below.

Lumber

The structure of wood is determined by the growth of the wood. A tree adds a layer of new growth every year. This growth appears as circu-lar rings on the ends of solid boards. (See Illus. 4-1.) These rings are more visible on some woods than on others.

These growth rings give boards patterns of lines on all surfaces. This is usually referred to as "grain." The grain, and the strength of the wood, usually runs with the length of the board. (See Illus. 4-1 and 4-2.) Try to cut your projects from the board so that it has as little "short grain" as possible.

The way growth rings appear in a board will also affect how easy it is to saw. Whether the blade has to cut vertically between them or perpen-dicularly through them will determine how easy it is to follow the layout line. Study the two boards shown in Illus. 4-1. Though they are the same wood, they are just cut differently from the tree.

Illus. 4-1. *Growth rings on Doug-las fir boards. Fir has one of the most extreme ranges of hardness and softness within each ring. This makes sawing difficult because the saw blade will tend to follow the softer areas of the board. Sawing the board on the left will be much more difficult than sawing the one on the right because of the ar-rangement of the growth rings. Avoid all boards with grain like that on the left; this type of wood is known as "quarter-sawn" wood.*

HARD

SOFT

As a general rule, beginners should avoid solid woods with prominent growth rings (grain figuration)—woods such as Southern pine, cedar, and redwood. Also, save or reserve expensive exotic woods only for very special projects, and only after you have gained experience with a scroll saw.

Softwoods such as pine are available at lumberyards. (See Illus. 4-3.) When buying lumber, remember that what lumber sellers call one-inch and two-inch-thick boards are really only ¾ and 1½ inches thick, respectively. A 2 × 4 is really only 1½ inches thick and 3½ inches wide. (See Illus. 4-4.)

Many hardwoods cut better and more smoothly than most softwoods. Poplar, mahogany, soft maple, and oak are hardwoods with good cutting qualities. (See Illus. 4-5.) These woods and some softwoods are often available in some building supply centers as pre-surfaced, smooth, ready-to-use boards that come in various sizes and of shorter lengths than typical building construction material.

Note: Before buying any quantity of wood or wood material, know exactly its quality.

Illus. 4-2. *The strength of wood is located along its length. Wood is more difficult to break across its length and grain pattern than it is with or parallel to it. Consequently, the project sawn at the left is more break-resistant than the one at the right, even though it was cut from the same board.*

Illus. 4-3. *Pine boards have a wide range of cutting characteristics. Avoid heavy boards. The heaviness may indicate high amounts of pitch or moisture. Boards with less distinct growth patterns or grain (figure), such as the one on the left, are easier to cut and are generally more serviceable overall.*

Illus. 4-4. *Carefully pick good-quality 2 × 4's (shown here), 2 × 6's, and 2 × 8's to use as inexpensive material for thicker cutouts. The lower piece is likely to cut more easily because of its more uniform density, which is typical of wood with less distinctive grain patterns.*

Illus. 4-5. *From left to right: Poplar, mahogany, soft maple, and oak. These hardwoods are good to use for scroll sawing.*

Sheet Material

The most widely used wood sheet material is plywood. Some projects and cutouts are best made from plywood, to minimize potential splitting or breaking. Plywood is made of thin layers of wood glued together, with the grain running at opposite directions in each layer.

Plywood has uniform strength (splitting resistance) lengthwise and widthwise. Plywood also has a uniform density and consistent cutting characteristics. Available plywood ranges in thickness from 1/32 inch up to 3/4 inch.

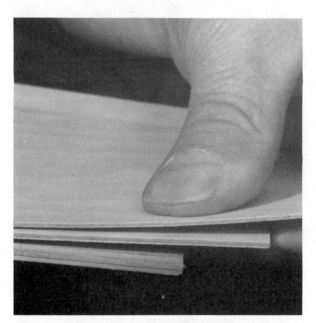

Illus. 4-6. *Plywood is made of hardwoods and softwoods and generally ranges in thickness from 1/32 inch to 3/4 inch. The most commonly used plywood is 1/4, 3/8, 1/2, and 3/4 inch thick.*

Illus. 4-7. *Some types of plywood are well-suited for scroll-sawing, and others aren't. This 3/4-inch-thick plywood Douglas fir splinters and breaks into slivers easily, making it a poor choice for toys, etc.*

Certain types of plywood are good for scroll-sawing. Other types aren't. (See Illus. 4-6–4-9.) Always use exterior plywood for outdoor projects.

One-quarter-inch thick hardwood plywood is good for thin cutouts, interior ornaments, etc., but scraps of plywood wall panelling, which is far more economical, easier to find, and in most cases prefinished, are ideal for the beginner. Professionals like Baltic or Finland birch plywood. (See Illus. 4-10.) It has more, thinner layers than typical plywood and cuts easily. It ranges in size up to ⅝ inch in thickness.

Hard, abrasive resins and glues are used in the manufacture of all sheet material. These resins and glues will eventually dull scroll-saw blades. The thicker the sheet material, the more quickly the blades will dull.

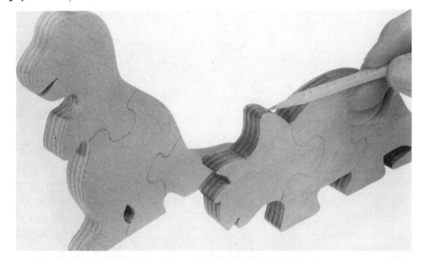

Illus. 4-8. *Some hardwood ply-woods do not splinter at all, but they have hard and abrasive glues that will dull blades very quickly and leave charred or burned sawn edges.*

Illus. 4-9. *Plywood is great to use for this project, to prevent break-age. If solid wood were used, it would have "short grain," regard-less of whether it is cut with the grain running vertically or horizontally.*

Illus. 4-10. *Some sheet materials, from left to right, are: medium-density fibreboard (MDF), wafer-board or chipboard, particle-board, hardboard, and Baltic birch plywood.*

Chapter 5

SAFETY TECHNIQUES

The first priority of any woodworker should be to avoid accidents. He should approach each cutting situation with the intention of properly following all safety techniques. And beginners, regardless of their age, should be taught to respect and care for their tools and equipment.

Even though the scroll saw is generally regarded as the safest of all woodworking tools, you should follow these safety rules:

1. Read and study the owner's manual. This will acquaint you with all of the mechanical features, their adjustments, and the general instructions for operating the saw.

2. Dress properly, for your own physical protection. (See Illus. 5-1.) Retain loose hair and tuck in any loose clothing. Remove dangling jewelry. Wear dust masks and goggles. These are especially important. This is because the dust blowers on many saws are more detrimental to the operator's health than they are helpful. They often drive the sawdust and microscopic particles generated by the fine-toothed scroll-saw blades right at the operator. (See Illus. 5-2 and 5-3.) In a half-hour of continuous sawing, a scroll-saw user may find his shirt covered with dust in the chest area. Some wood dusts are toxic, and some individuals might be allergic to the dust from certain woods such as cedar.

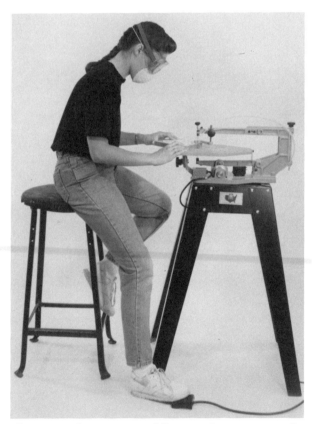

Illus. 5-1. *This woman is following the proper scroll-sawing safety techniques: she is not wearing loose clothing or jewelry, her hair is pulled back, and she is wearing goggles and a dust mask. Note also that the height of the stool she is sitting on allows her to sit with a straight back, she is using both a foot switch and a hold-down, and that the area is well lighted.*

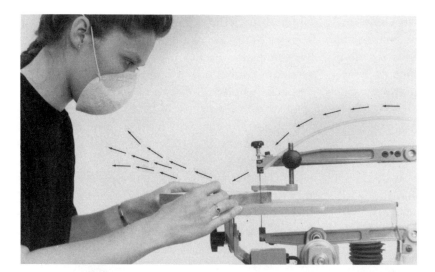

Illus. 5-2. *The biggest problem with nearly every commercial scroll saw's dust-blower system is that it blows all fine particles and sawdust directly at the operator. Note the use of a dust mask for respiratory protection.*

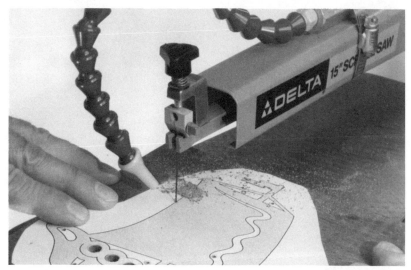

Illus. 5-3. *This shop-made blower system is excellent in that it blows the sawdust away from the operator. Refer to page 41 for more information on this setup.*

Illus. 5-4. *Beginners should use the hold-down, adjusted properly for the workpiece thickness so that it doesn't move up and down on the worktable.*

3. Use whatever safety-related devices are provided by the manufacturer, such as guards and hold-downs, until you are sure that you can safely work without them in certain cutting situations where they will interfere with the work. (See Illus. 5-4 and 5-5.)

Some machines do not provide guards that cover the upper arms. When using these machines, be especially careful that you don't get your hands or fingers caught between the workpiece and the oscillating arm. (See Illus. 5-6.) Avoid placing your hands and fingers under the upper arm of the saw. Also, never reach under the saw table or saw base while the saw is running.

There are accessories available that will help you use your scroll saw more safely. One that is especially helpful, convenient, and saves time is a foot switch. (See Illus. 5-7.) A foot switch is helpful because if you ever have a problem during a cut, you do not have to remove your hands to shut off the switch.

Other accessories that will prove helpful are lighting attachments and combination lights and magnifiers that attach to the saw. These accessories will help ensure that the cutting area is well-

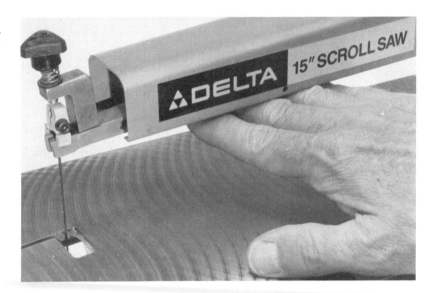

Illus. 5-5. *Some saws come with upper arm guards, which are good devices. Beginners should keep the upper arm guards on their saws, and use them.*

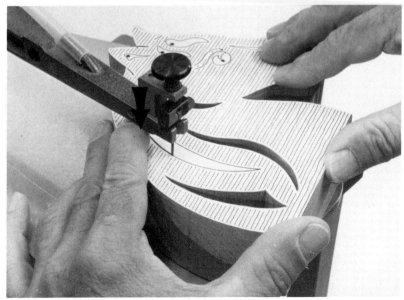

Illus. 5-6. *Make sure that your hands or fingers do not get battered or pinched between the oscillating upper arm and the workpiece. Be especially cautious when sawing thick material, as shown here.*

Illus. 5-7. *A foot switch is regarded as a safety accessory because both of the operator's hands are freed to hold down and control the work.*

6. Do not operate the saw in moist or damp environments.

7. Always install the blades with their teeth pointing forward and downward.

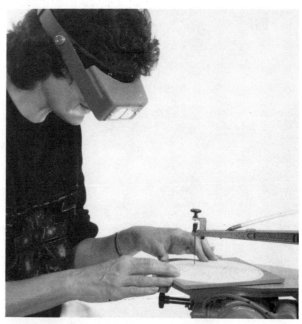

Illus. 5-8. *This headband-type magnifier works with and without glasses. It can be tilted up when not needed.*

lighted and without shadows, which is essential. Some professionals, however, do not like to mount lights and magnifiers directly onto their saws. This is because the vibration caused by the machine creates for them an uncomfortable sense of movement.

Also available are headpiece magnifiers that can be used with regular glasses. (See Illus. 5-8 and 5-9.) These magnifiers are very helpful for individuals with vision problems and those who do highly detailed work.

4. Be aware of the potential danger in certain cutting situations. You may find that you will have to place your fingers very close to the sides of the blade to control or hold down the workpiece. (See Illus. 5-10–5-12.) Avoid such situations and situations where you have to cut very small pieces, until you have become thoroughly familiar with the way the saw cuts, and are sure that you can control it.

5. Make sure that the machine is properly grounded with an appropriate three-prong electrical plug and grounded receptacle.

Illus. 5-9. *These small clip-on magnifiers available from optical centers can be attached to glasses.*

Illus. 5-10. *When possible, press your fingertips downward on the stock and push your thumbs against the edge of the stock, advancing it into the saw as shown above. Note that both hands are well away from the cutting area, but still in complete control.*

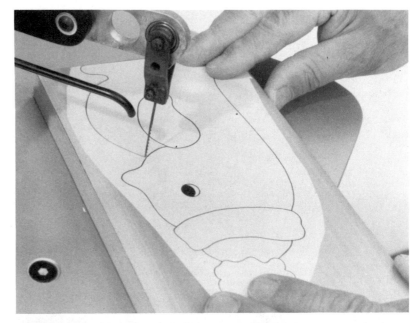

Illus. 5-11. *Sometimes it's necessary to place your fingers close to the blade to hold down or control the stock. However,* **never** *place your fingers in the cutting path of the saw blade.*

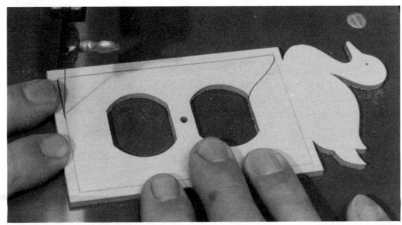

Illus. 5-12. *When you have to put your fingers close to the blade to exert pressure on the workpiece, it is better to put them behind the blade (as with the left index finger shown here) rather than immediately to the near side or in front of the blade.*

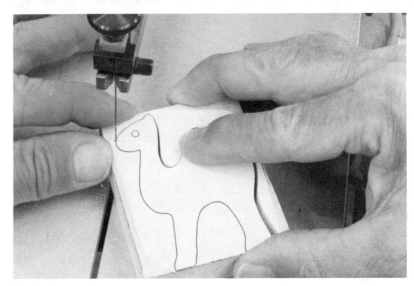

8. Make sure that you have adjusted the table tilt, the hold-down, and the blade to its correct tension before turning on the power.

9. Do not leave the machine unattended with the power on.

10. Do not use any tools while under the influence of medication, drugs, alcohol, or when fatigued.

11. Only use sharp blades. Never use blades that are dull or bent.

12. Until you have gained some experience, only cut materials that lay flat on the table. Do not cut round dowels, tubing, etc.

13. Do not cut curves or radiuses that are too tight (sharp) for the width of blade being used.

14. If the saw has speed choice options, beginners should use the slower speed.

15. Release the blade tension when you are finished sawing.

16. Keep your tools and work area clean.

17. Lock master switches or power sources to keep idle tools from being used by unauthorized individuals.

18. Before starting the cut, visualize all the steps involved in the cutting process.

Chapter 6

SETTING UP THE SAW

There are several things that must be done to the saw before it can be used to make cuts. These procedures include: installing the blade, tensioning the blade, squaring the saw table to the blade, adjusting the hold-down, and, in some cases, changing (reducing) the blade's cutting speed to an optimum level. These adjustments are easy to make, and quickly become part of your routine.

Clamping and Installing the Blade

As discussed in Chapter 1, each brand of saw has its own type of blade-suspension and clamping system. Each system is adjusted differently. Consult your owner's manual for specific procedures.

Once you have selected a blade, be sure that it will be installed so that its teeth point forward and downwards. Beginners should start with a blade that is not smaller than a No. 7 or No. 8 blade. A No. 9 or No. 11 blade is highly recommended.

To clamp and install the blade, first secure the blade clamps to the ends of the blade as recommended in the owner's manual. Some saws provide a special "built-in" blade-clamp-holding fixture(s) that makes this procedure easier. Your saw will probably have a blade-changing system like one of the systems that can be found on a Sakura,

Hegner, RBI, Sears, or Dremel saw. These systems are shown and described in Illus. 6-1–6-7.

Illus. 6-8–6-10 show and explain how to clamp the lower blade clamp to the lower arm so that the blade will extend vertically through the table. Make sure that the blade clamps sit (or are seated) in their proper locations on their respective arms. At first you should check this visually, but after you have gained some experience you will be able to do this without looking, by feeling with your thumb and fingers. Once the blade clamps are seated, begin tensioning the blade.

Illus. 6-1. *The blade-changing fixture on Sakura saws is to the side of the hold-down arm.*

Illus. 6-2. *The Hegner blade-clamping fixture is attached to the table, and holds everything steady as the blade clamp is tightened to the blade.*

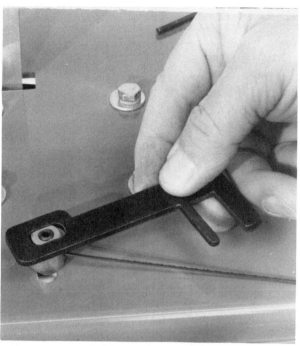

Illus. 6-4. *The F wrench is used to tighten the blade in the lower blade holder as it is held in the slot in the saw base.*

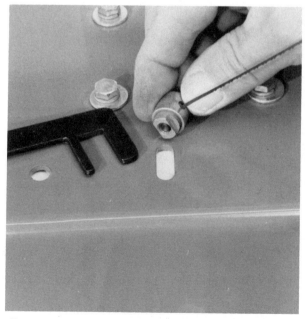

Illus. 6-3. *The lower blade clamp on RBI saws fits into a slot in the saw base that matches the "flats"— the two flat areas or surfaces on the lower blade clamp. The blade is inserted through a hole in the outer bronze bearing and secured in the clamp with the special wrench shown at the left.*

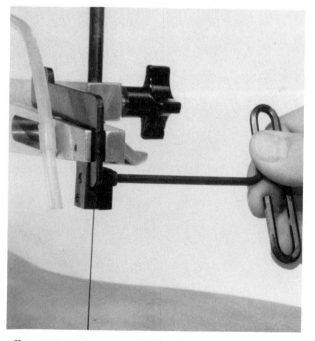

Illus. 6-5. *Tightening a blade clamp on the upper arm of an RBI Hawk saw. Here the F wrench steadies the pivoting parallel-jaw blade clamp as it is tightened.*

Illus. 6-6. *The blade-changing fixtures on Dremel saws are cast onto the overarm guard housing.*

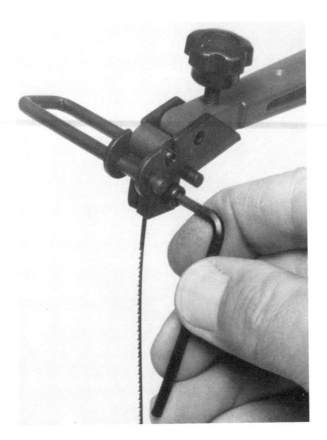

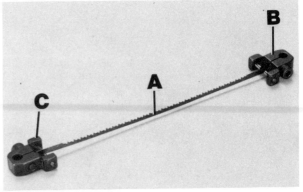

Illus. 6-8. *Whatever blade-suspension system your saw has, the blade (A) must be clamped at both ends (B and C) with loose or separate blade clamps or with non-removable blade clamps that are always attached to one or both arms of the saw.*

Illus. 6-7. *The Sears and Delta 16-inch saws have a similar "U"-shaped bar (at the left) that steadies the blade clamp as it is tightened or loosened. The tensioning adjustments on this Sears saw and Delta's 16- and 18-inch saws are located up front.*

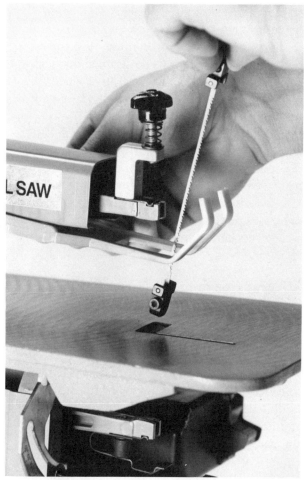

Illus. 6-9. *When you have released the blade's tension on the upper arm, place the blade clamps into their proper positions on the ends of the upper and lower arms. Here the bottom blade clamp is being lowered through an opening in the table to get it onto the lower saw arm.*

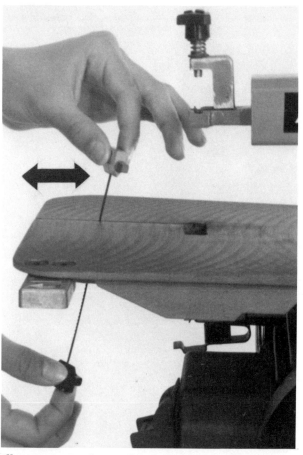

Illus. 6-10. *On this modified 15-inch saw, which has a user-made full-to-the-edge table slot, the blade and blade-clamp assembly slide in easily from the front, just as it is done when making blade changes on the more expensive Hegner saws.*

Tensioning the Blade

Blade tensioning controls may be found at the rear of the upper arm (Illus. 6-11) or located on the front of the upper arm (Illus. 6-7).

Judging the right amount of blade tension will be slightly tricky for the beginner. Larger blades can take more pressure than narrower ones. However, too little tension, on any size blade, will cause the blade to "drift" in the saw cut. This means that it will be difficult when feeding the workpiece to keep cutting on the layout line as desired. The blade will have a tendency to wander off or drift from side to side as it follows the grain. A cut that drifts vertically is also undesirable. It will produce a sawn surface that bulges or results in a cut that is not true or square to the saw table.

Another indication of too little blade tension is excessive machine noise and vibration. A properly tensioned saw will run more quietly. Conversely, too much tension will cause narrower blades (No. 5 and less) to break prematurely.

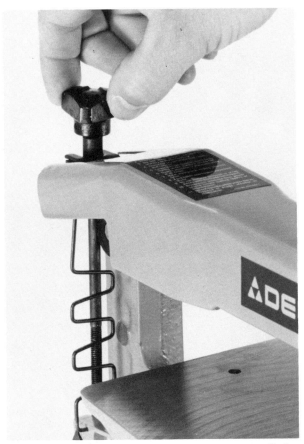

Illus. 6-11. *Blade tension on most saws is controlled at the rear of the upper arm. Clockwise rotation increases, and counterclockwise rotation lessens, tension.*

There are two different ways to determine the optimum blade tension. Both require judgment by the operator. In one method, the operator checks the tension by physically pushing against the front of the blade with a scrap of wood. (See Illus. 6-12.) If the blade is properly tensioned, it will deflect or bend ⅛ or 3/16 inch with a certain amount of pressure. In the second, which is perhaps the more widely used, the operator repeatedly plucks the blade (as he would pluck a guitar string), while simultaneously increasing the tension. (See Illus. 6-13.) When the blade is at a point where it is properly tensioned or stiffened, it will impart a certain sound.

Squaring the Table

It is extremely important that you adjust the saw table so that it is perfectly square or at right angles to the properly installed and tensioned blade. A table that is not at right angles to the blade will result in a bevel or angular cut, which, unless it is intentional, can present major problems in certain situations. For example, if you are sawing toy puzzles out of a piece of wood, they may not disassemble or come apart the way they should if the pieces are not cut on a perfectly squared table.

Illus. 6-12. *One way to check tension with medium-to-large blades is to exert moderate pressure to the front of the blade (using a block, as shown) to cause a deflection or bend. If the blade deflects about ⅛ to 3/16 inch, it is properly tensioned. Note the bend in the blade in this photo.*

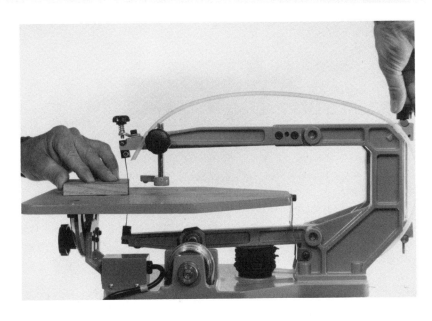

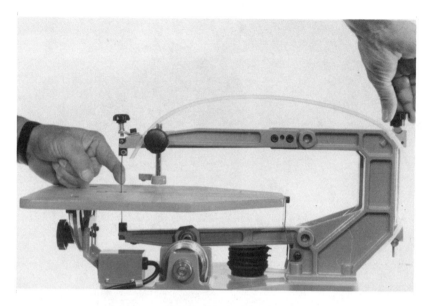

Illus. 6-13. *Another popular way to check blade tension is to repeatedly pluck the blade with your index finger with one hand while turning the tension knob clockwise with your other hand.*

To square the table, release the table-tilt lock knob by turning it counterclockwise (opposite the direction in which a clock's hands move), and then retighten it with a clockwise turn. (See Illus. 6-14.) Use a combination square to check that the table is square with the side of tensioned blade. (See Illus. 6-15 and 6-16.)

You can also square the table quickly without a hand square. This simple procedure, involving some trial and error with a block of wood, is shown in Illus. 6-17–6-20.

Illus. 6-14. *Loosen the table-tilting control knob by turning it counterclockwise.*

Illus. 6-15. *Use a combination square to check that the table is square with the blade. To do this, look at the blade and see how it lines up with the edge of the square.*

Illus. 6-16. *A larger square can also be used. Simply sight along its edge from a position that is directly in front of the saw.*

Illus. 6-17. *Squaring the table without a hand square. Step A. Make a cut into the edge of a fairly thick piece of wood.*

Illus. 6-18. *Step B. Turn the piece of wood around and bring it up behind the blade so that the direction of the cut made in the edge can be compared to the blade.*

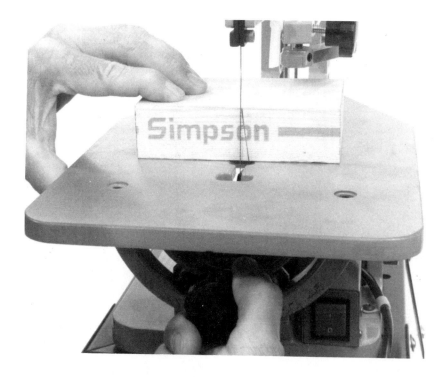

Illus. 6-19. *Step C. The amount of table-tilt adjustment needed to make the table square with the blade is just one-half of the angle made between the line of the blade and the line of the cut made into the edge of the wood. Reset the table to this amount.*

Illus. 6-20. *Step D. Make another cut, as done in Step A (Illus. 6-17), and compare it again with the blade. Repeat as necessary, until the blade lines up perfectly with its corresponding cut. The table is now perfectly square to the tensioned blade.*

Adjusting the Hold-down

Place the piece of wood to be cut flat on the table near the side or the front of the blade. If the workpiece varies in its thickness or the board is twisted (warped), move the hold-down to the highest area or part of the workpiece it should be at. (See Illus. 6-21.) This is necessary so that the work will fit under it and will not be restricted when it is fed into the moving blade. Better hold-downs are slightly flexible, to accommodate minor changes in stock thickness while you are sawing.

Illus. 6-21. *Adjust the hold-down to fit the thickness of the wood.*

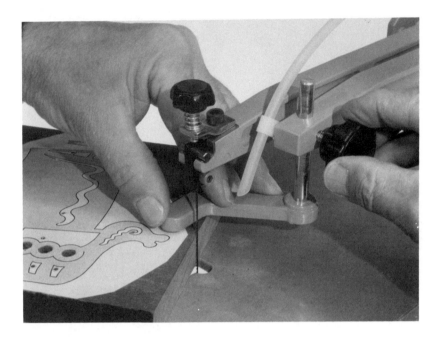

Setting Blade Speeds

Saws that provide the operator with a choice of blade speeds in strokes per minute (spm) should be used at the outset. And though it benefits a scroll sawyer to cut as quickly as possible, beginners should use slow speeds when possible, regardless of stock thickness, amount of cutting detail, or the hardness of the material to be cut. As you become more experienced, you will not have any difficulty determining the optimum cutting speed for whatever sawing job you may be confronted with. Consult the owner's manual for specific recommendations as to which speeds to use in certain situations and how to adjust your saw to such speeds.

Chapter 7
PATTERNS

Types and Sources of Patterns

Patterns are drawings that outline the shape of the object you want to cut. Ready-to-use scroll-saw commercial patterns are available for making shapes that range from very simple cutouts (Illus. 7-1) to highly detailed and complicated pieces of fine fretwork (Illus. 7-3). Special books full of ready-to-trace or copy designs are very popular,

and economically provide many good patterns. Sterling Publishing Company (387 Park Avenue South, New York, New York 10016) sells many of these types of books. Various companies also sell individual pattern sheets.

Full-size, ready-to-use patterns are the easiest to work with. However, the modern office photocopier now has enlarging and reducing capabilities, so it's easier than ever to prepare and copy patterns in any size desired.

Good patterns—especially the more complex ones—should have sharp, crisp lines with some

Illus. 7-1. *Examples of high-quality patterns. Note the examples of good shading, which is softer and will contrast with the saw blade. Patterns with line shading (lower left and right) usually suggest which way to place the pattern on the wood with regard to its grain direction. Also note the crisp, thin outlines and smooth-flowing curves.*

Illus. 7-2. *The shaded pattern on the right will be much easier to saw. It is less confusing because it clearly distinguishes which areas are to be cut away.*

Illus. 7-3. *Fully blackened patterns such as these are less desirable than those with light-grey or line-shaded areas. On highly detailed work such as this your eyes become weary distinguishing the dark saw blade from the dark areas on the pattern.*

Illus. 7-4. *Crude patterns such as these are quickly identified by thick, sloppy line work, lack of shading, and crude and uninteresting designs.*

Illus. 7-5. *Beginners should select project patterns that are easiest to cut. It is more difficult to cut the letters at the left than to cut those at the right. If the letters at the left are not sawn perfectly (the straight lines perfectly straight, and the sharp corners sharp), any inaccuracies will be highly visible. The letters at the right will look good even if not sawn precisely.*

Illus. 7-6. *These decals, applied directly to the wood and cut out as shown, make quick, colorful, well-designed puzzles for children. See the book* Scroll Saw Puzzle Patterns *for more ideas.*

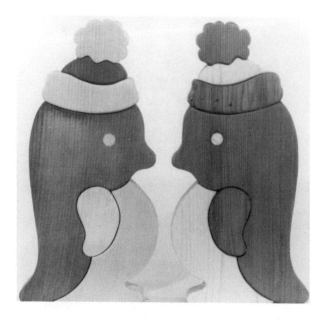

soft tone shading, to minimize eyestrain when sawing. (See Illus. 7-2 and 7-3.) The pattern should provide some visual contrast to the thin, dark saw blade.

Many patterns are not prepared carefully, have crude designs, and simply do not suit the basic needs of the scroll-sawyer. (See Illus. 7-4.)

Beginners should select patterns of designs that are not too complex or demanding. (See Illus.

Illus. 7-7. *A cutout pattern (left), and one cut out in reverse. These projects are examples of segmentation or basic intarsia. In these techniques, individual pieces are sawn from different woods, or from the same piece of wood and stained differently, and then glued together.*

7-5.) If the pattern outlines on some designs are not followed precisely, the overall visual appearance will still look good. Miscuts will not be apparent to the casual observer.

The creative scroll-saw user can find good sources for his favorite kinds of patterns and designs. Wallpaper, coloring books, stickers, decals (Illus. 7-6), gift wrappings, and greeting cards, often have suitable profiles that make great sawing patterns.

time until the entire pattern is completed and drawn to a new size. This technique, along with the technique of using a pantograph (an inexpensive proportioning instrument), is described in the *Scroll Saw Handbook*. These methods are now more or less obsolete because of the office photocopier. If you don't have access to a photocopier, you may want to hand-trace patterns onto thin, transparent paper, rather than remove pages from books.

Enlarging and Reducing Patterns

As mentioned, full-sized, enlarged, or reduced copies can best be made on the modern office photocopy machine. Some machines also have the capability of printing directly onto clear, thin plastic, which can, in turn, be used to create reverse patterns. A reverse-image pattern is sometimes useful for special projects. (See Illus. 7-7.)

There are other, more traditional, ways of enlarging and reducing patterns. These include the graph square or grid technique, which involves freehand drawing of one small, squared area at a

Transferring the Patterns

There are many ways the lines of the pattern or pattern copies can be applied to the surface of the wood. One conventional technique is to hand-trace a pattern placed over carbon or graphite paper. (See Illus. 7-8.) Always check to be sure all lines are traced and transferred to the wood before removing or shifting the position of the pattern. Graphite transfer paper is better because it can be cleaned off the wood more easily than the

Illus. 7-8. *The traditional method of transferring a copy of a pattern freehand involves the use of carbon or graphite paper, with the pattern taped on top.*

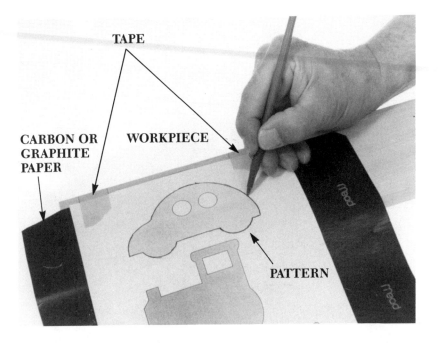

"greasy" carbon papers. White and dark graphite papers are available in various sizes from arts and crafts supply stores. (See Illus. 7-9 and 7-10.)

When tracing with transfer papers or making layouts directly onto the wood, use circle templates, a compass, or a straightedge to ensure accurate layouts. Freehand-tracing is simply not a good way to transfer accurate lines for sawing. (See Illus. 7-11–7-13.)

The fastest, most accurate, and easiest way to apply a pattern to the surface of the wood is to temporarily bond it directly to the workpiece. Two kinds of adhesive are commonly used: rubber cement and a special spray adhesive with temporary bonding qualities. The author prefers the latter, and uses 3-M's Scotch™ Spray Mount™ Artist's Adhesive #6065, but there are other brands available.

Illus. 7-9. *If you must trace a pattern freehand, use white graphite paper (right), for more visible layouts on dark woods.*

Illus. 7-10. *The photocopied pattern applied directly to the wood at right obviously provides smoother, crisper, and more accurate sawing lines than can be achieved with carbon or graphite paper tracings, as shown at the left.*

Illus. 7-11. *All circles and arcs should be laid out with a template or a compass.*

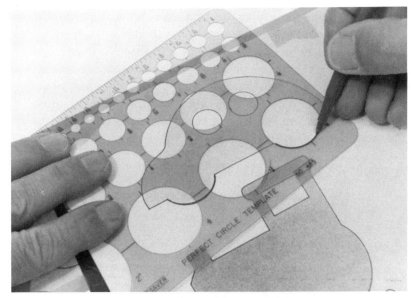

Illus. 7-12. *When transferring a layout pattern manually, as shown here with carbon paper, use a straightedge for straight lines.*

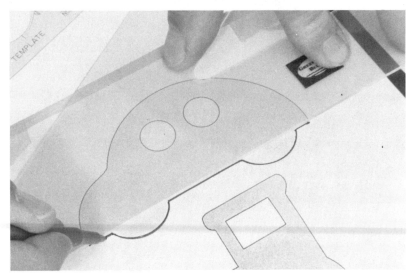

Illus. 7-13. *Accurate layouts and pattern transfers are important. At left: a pattern copied by hand with carbon paper. At center, a pattern copied by hand with the aid of a circle template and straightedge. At right, a photocopy of the pattern applied directly to the wood, obviously the best approach.*

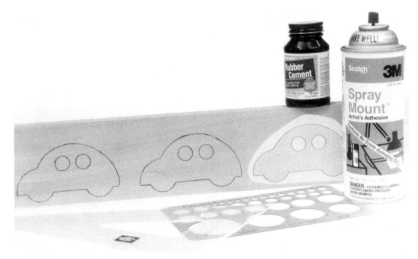

When using either rubber cement or the spray adhesive, apply it to the back of the pattern copy, not directly to the wood. Apply just a very light brush coating or spray a light "mist" of the spray adhesive. Wait a few seconds until the adhesive is tacky, and press the pattern onto the wood. (See Illus. 7-14–7-16.) You are ready to start sawing.

After the sawing is completed, you can peel the pattern off very easily. (See Illus. 7-17.) The spray adhesive leaves little residue on the surface, and does not inhibit subsequent finishing. If any rubber cement remains, rub it off with your fingers.

There are two other ways to transfer the lines of patterns copied with a photocopier directly onto the wood: the iron-on technique and the solvent transfer method. (See Illus. 7-18–7-21.) These techniques have some limitations, and both result in reversed images, which may or may not be acceptable.

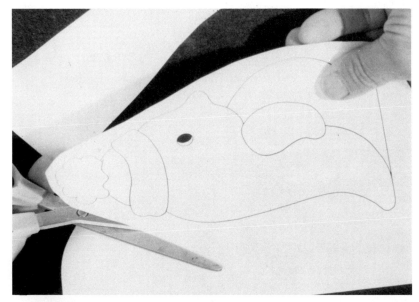

Illus. 7-14. *Roughly cut around the photocopied pattern with a pair of scissors.*

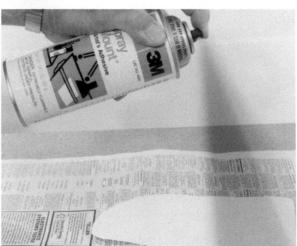

Illus. 7-15. *Apply a very light "mist" of spray adhesive only to the back of the pattern. Do not spray directly onto the wood. Note that a newspaper underneath the pattern is being used to catch the overspray.*

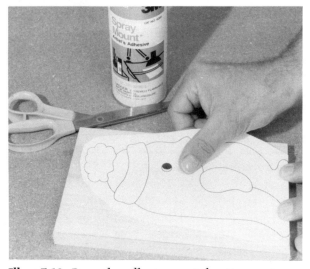

Illus. 7-16. *Press the adhesive-coated pattern onto the workpiece. Note that in this case the bottom straight edge of the pattern is aligned with the previously sawn straight edge of the wood.*

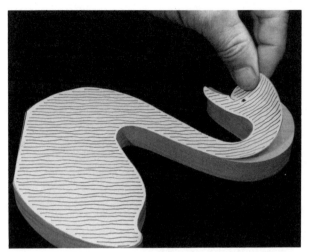

Illus. 7-17. *After you have completed the sawing, you can lift the pattern from the wood cleanly and easily.*

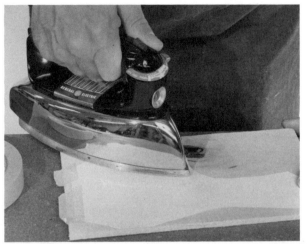

Illus. 7-18. *Patterns copied with an office machine can be transferred directly to the wood with a flat-iron, as shown. The pattern will be reversed, however. See Illus. 7-19.*

Using Templates

A template is a thin, durable material cut to the exact size and shape of the desired part. (See Illus. 7-22 and 7-23.) To lay out the pattern with a template simply trace the template along its edges with a sharp pencil (not a pen) on the material to be cut.

A half-template is recommended where the pattern can be split down the middle and both sides are the same, as for example, a heart-shaped pattern. The half-template is flipped over to lay out both sides.

Laying Out Circles, Arcs, and Ovals

Circles, arcs, and ovals are best drawn with the aid of a compass, template, or any other means that will provide a perfectly smooth curve to follow with the saw. (See Illus. 7-24.) Sometimes it is better to draw circles, arcs, and ovals directly onto the wood, rather than attempt to make your own pattern or template.

Ovals are visually pleasing if laid out with good length-to-width proportions. Some common

ratios are 2×3, 3×5, 5×7, 8×10, and 11×14. The simple steps for drawing perfect ovals are shown in Illus. 7-25–7-29.

Illus. 7-19. *The resulting ironed-on pattern is a reversal of the original. Sometimes as many as four transfers can be made this way, but each successive one is less clear.*

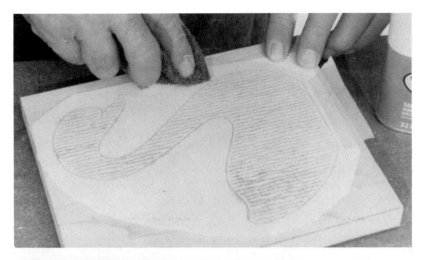

Illus. 7-20. *A photocopied pattern can also be transferred with a cloth pad and lacquer thinner solvent. This technique is less favorable because of the toxic, explosive fumes of the lacquer-thinner.*

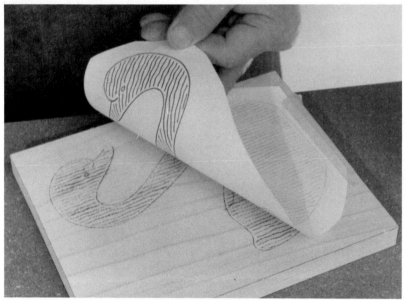

Illus. 7-21. *Solvent-transferred patterns, like those ironed on, appear reversed on the wood. Certain patterns such as letters and numbers obviously cannot be used.*

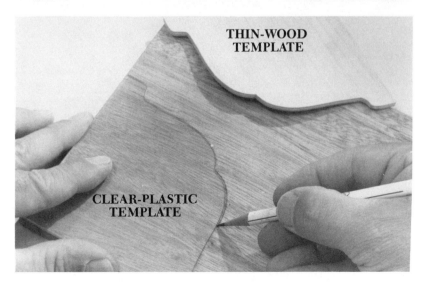

Illus. 7-22. *Templates cut from thin wood, cardboard, soft sheet metals, and clear plastic are good for transferring patterns to the wood. Clear plastic can be seen through, which helps you to determine the best location on the wood to place the pattern. This is away from knots, stains, cracks, and other defects. Here a corner shelf project is laid out flush with a previously squared corner.*

Illus. 7-23. *Think about making templates for future use when sawing out a project. Here a thin piece of tagboard has been sandwiched between two pieces of wood (tacked together) and cut, to make a reusable template.*

Illus. 7-24. *Washers and coins often make good templates for making circles and rounding corners, as shown here.*

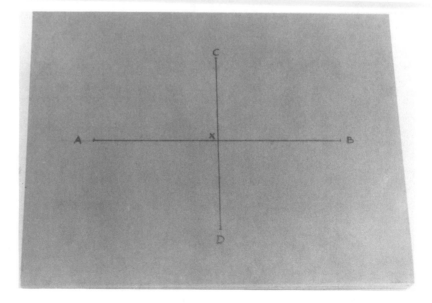

Illus. 7-25. *Step A. The first step in laying out a true ellipse or oval. A-B equals the major diameter. C-D equals the minor diameter, which bisects and is laid out perpendicular (at right angles) to A-B at X.*

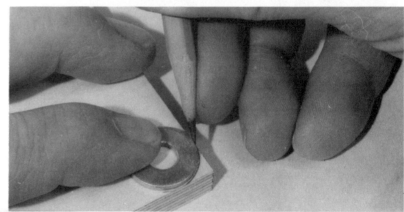

Illus. 7-26. *Step B. Set a divider (or compass) to half the major diameter, as shown.*

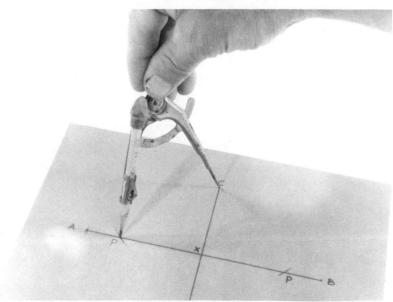

Illus. 7-27. *Step C. With C as the base (center) point, set off P-P on line A-B. C-P is equal to A-X (that is, it is ½ the distance of the major diameter).*

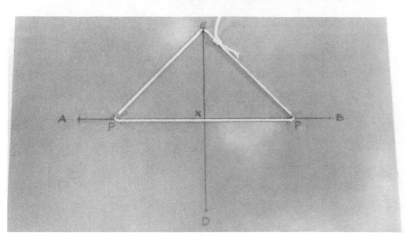

Illus. 7-28. *Step D. Set nails, tacks, or pins at P-P and point C. Pull a string tightly around these three points and tie it securely. Remove the pin or tack at point C.*

Illus. 7-29. *Step E. Keep the string as taut as possible with a pencil, as shown, and, while simultaneously moving the pencil around, draw a perfectly true oval.*

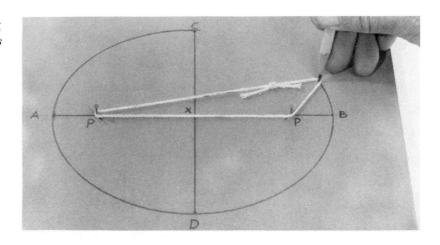

Effective Layout Tips

Good wood is expensive and scarce, and all woodworkers should avoid waste whenever possible. (See Illus. 7-30.) Illus. 7-31–7-33 provide some helpful ideas for conserving wood with effective layout methods.

Illus. 7-30. *Pattern layouts such as this one waste valuable wood material.*

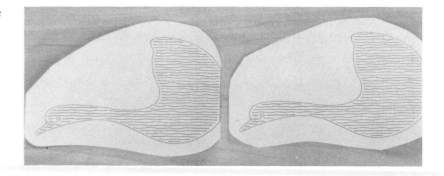

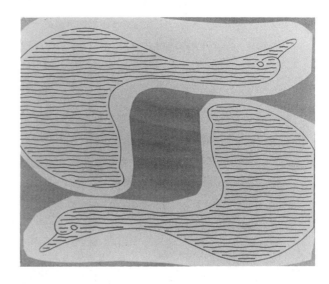

Illus. 7-31. *A better, more conservative use of material.*

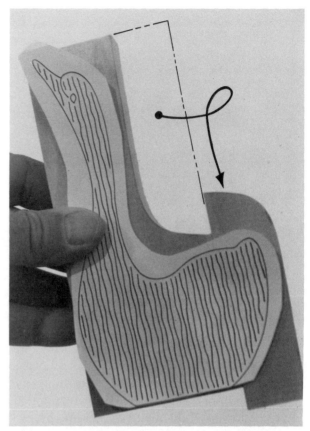

Illus. 7-33. *The waste piece is glued on. With this technique, you can make a cutout from a board originally narrower than the pattern. Note: as a rule, boards can be glued to increase their width and thickness, but not glued end to end to increase their length.*

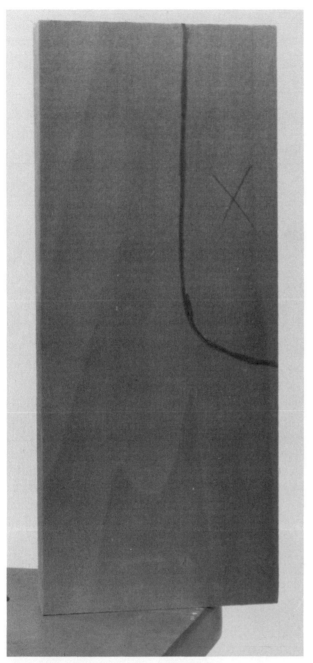

Illus. 7-32. *The waste by the narrow area of the pattern, as shown by the X, is cut away and used to widen the lower, wide area of the pattern. See Illus. 7-33.*

Chapter 8
MAKING BASIC CUTS

All scroll-sawing routinely involves cutting any one or a combination of the following: irregular curved lines; straight lines; sharp corners and angles; and regular curves (true arcs and perfect circles). Once the skills to perform these cuts freehand (without aids or mechanical guides) are mastered, 95 percent of all scroll-sawing jobs will be extremely easy.

This chapter explores the fundamentals involved in making these basic cuts and other basic sawing techniques. (Illus. 8-1 is a pattern on which to practise some of these techniques.) The chapters that follow deal with techniques and methods that are used in conjunction with the skills learned here.

Preparing for Sawing

Before using a scroll saw, a beginner should become familiar with the way it sounds and feels. It is important to recognize and get used to the normal sound of the machine when it is running freely (not cutting) and also when it is under load cutting wood. If the saw sounds differently when running under these conditions, this is an indication of possible problems, such as a blade that is not properly tensioned, slipping blade clamps, or even bearing failure. In such a case, shut off the power, investigate, and correct the problem immediately.

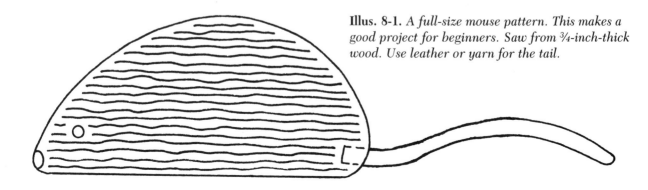

Illus. 8-1. *A full-size mouse pattern. This makes a good project for beginners. Saw from ¾-inch-thick wood. Use leather or yarn for the tail.*

Cutting Irregular Curves

After you have become familiar with the saw, adjust it to a slow speed, if possible, and prepare to make practice cuts. Select inexpensive ¾-inch-thick or medium-thick softwood of a reasonable length and width. Without using layout lines, cut gentle curves straight across the grain. Then cut gentle curves with the grain. Feed the stock slowly but steadily directly into the front of the blade. Turn the stock left or right, as required to make the desired curve. You'll make these observations:

1. The wood cuts easier across the grain than with it.

2. The blade will bend rearwards slightly. This is nothing to be concerned with. Slowing the feed rate will return the blade to a straight and vertical position again.

3. A slower feed produces a smooth finish and squarer cuts. This is an important point to remember when making sharper or tighter turns, especially in thick or harder woods.

After you have transferred or applied the pattern to the wood, you are ready to make a cutout. Patterns often have irregular curves that have to be cut out. Remember these two points when making a cutout.

1. If the object must be sawn from a larger board, cut it out to a rough shape first, so that it's at a size that's easier to handle. (See Illus. 8-2.)

2. When cutting patterns with straight edges, such as the base or bottom of the mouse pattern shown in Illus. 8-1, it often saves time and material and is easier to position the pattern to the edge of the board. This is because the part of the pattern on the edge of the board will not have to be cut at all. (See Illus. 8-3–8-5.)

Illus. 8-2. *If the project must be cut from a large board, first cut it out to its rough shape, as shown, so that it's at a more workable size.*

Illus. 8-3. *An example of good hand position during sawing. The fingers hold the stock down by pressing on its surface. The thumbs grip the edge of the work-piece. Note that the cut is made right on the line.*

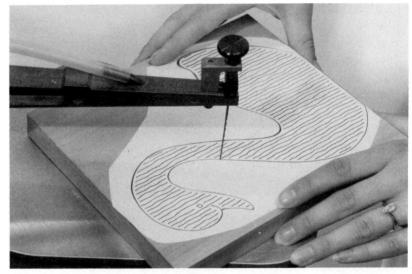

Illus. 8-4. *Making a smaller cut-out. Note the same thumb and finger positions. Also, note that the left index finger is placed safely behind the blade.*

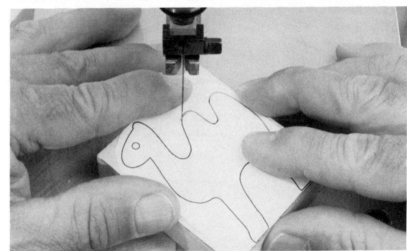

Illus. 8-5. *The straight edge of the pattern is placed on the edge of the board. At the very start of the cut, align just the first ¹⁄₁₆ to ⅛ inch of the curved layout line with an imaginary cutting line of the blade that extends from the front through the rear of the blade; this is indicated by the dotted line. This will help you see where to begin your cut, and help to feed the workpiece in the right direction. Feed the work directly into the front of the blade. In this case, the operator is starting the cut by advancing the stock into the blade in a clockwise direction.*

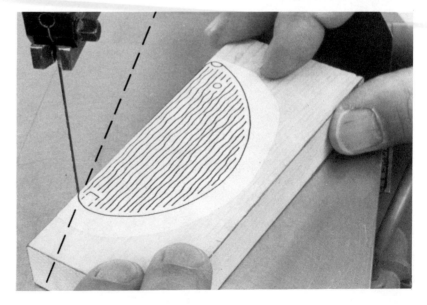

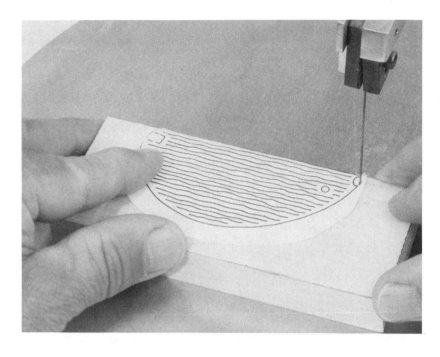

Illus. 8-6. *Cutting with a counter-clockwise feeding direction. There is no one recommended feeding direction. Sooner or later you will find it necessary to feed the stock into the blade in either direction—clockwise or counterclockwise.*

You can begin cutting a cutout by feeding the workpiece in either a clockwise or counterclockwise direction. (See Illus. 8-5 and 8-6.) Eventually, you will be skillful enough to saw in both directions, so it does not matter which direction you choose.

It is important, however, that you learn initially to cut on the line or just to the outside of it. (See Illus. 8-7–8-10.) Always avoid cutting to the inside of the pattern line. This eliminates any opportunity to correct a cut if it has not been made precisely, and should be precise.

Beginners should try to select cutouts with design profiles that do not have to be precisely cut. (See Illus. 8-10.)

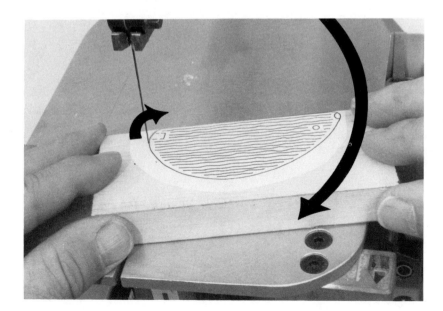

Illus. 8-7. *As you slowly feed the workpiece to make the small curve at the beginning of the cut, the opposite end of the stock will be rotated rather quickly and move a good distance, as shown by the large arrow. Note the positions of the thumb and fingers on the workpiece.*

Illus. 8-8. *Try to feed the wood so that the cut will be made on the line or just outside of it. Always avoid cutting inside the line. Should you veer off, cutting too far away from the line, do not try to correct it quickly or you'll have a noticeable bump on what is supposed to be a smoothly flowing curve.*

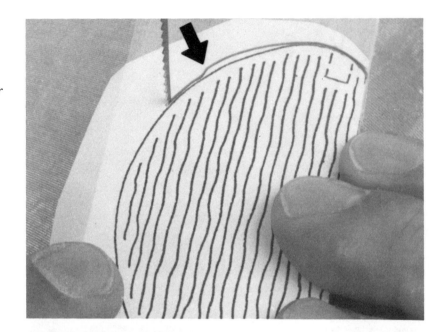

Illus. 8-9. *"Fairing out" the curve by gradually cutting back to the line. Even though the object is not cut perfectly to the line, no one will ever know. Notice the thumb and finger positions at this point of the cut. The right index finger acts somewhat as a pivot point.*

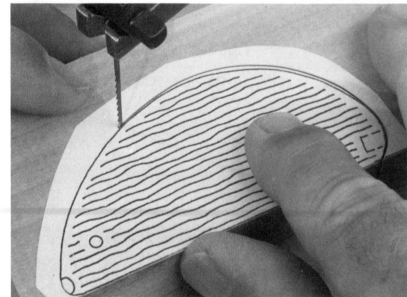

Illus. 8-10. *Two mouse cutouts, neither perfectly sawn. Which looks better, the one with the "faired" curve, at the left, or the one with the "bump," at the right? Beginners should start with designs that do not have to be precisely cut, such as this mouse project.*

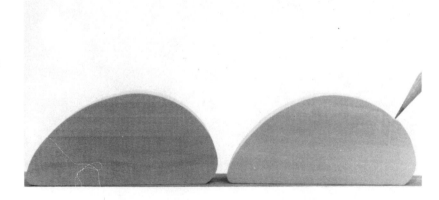

Cutting Straight Lines

It is better to cut straight lines freehand, by following the lines just as you would when cutting curves. The fences, mitre gauges, and similar mechanical devices used on table saws and band saws do not function effectively when used on scroll saws. One reason is that the much narrower blade used on scroll saws tends to follow the wood's grain. Another is the fact that scroll-saw blades do not have set teeth that dig in on both sides of the cut equally.

Also, remember that scroll-saw blades have a burr that runs along one edge of the teeth, usually on the right side as you face the saw blade. This means that one side of the blade cuts differently than the other, requiring a slight compensation in feed direction. To follow a straight layout line, you must adjust the feed of the material slightly, just a few degrees more to the right as you face the saw. (See Illus. 8-11–8-13.)

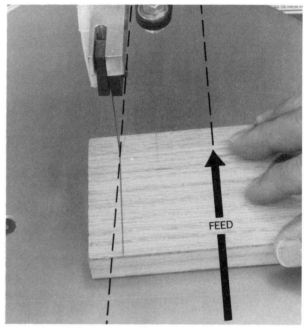

Illus. 8-11. *When straight-line sawing, you have to feed the workpiece slightly more to the right of the blade in order to keep the blade following the line. The perceived line of cut is the line to the left. The feed must be at a slight angle to it, as indicated by the feed direction line at the right.*

Illus. 8-12. *Take "aim" before beginning a straight-line cut. Position the workpiece so that the cut will be on course immediately as the cut begins. Proper stock positioning and feeding will become easier with experience.*

Illus. 8-13. *Feed the stock forward uniformly with both hands. Stop feeding it when you have to change directions. When making a corner cut, "aim" before continuing the cut.*

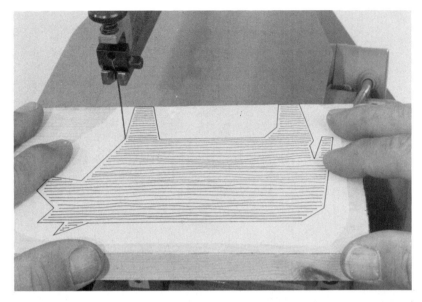

Illus. 8-14. *Inside corners, which are less than 90 degrees to the blade, are fairly easy to handle with narrow blades. Here a No. 7 blade can make the quick turn to change the cutting direction, so that the cut can be continued without interruption.*

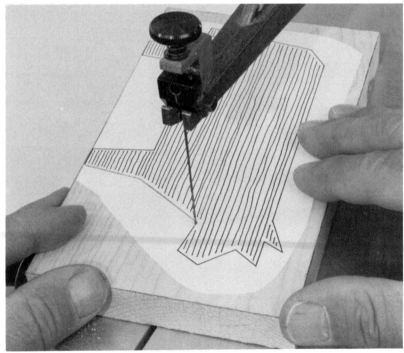

Making Sharp Turns and Corner Cuts

The scroll saw can make extremely sharp turns without difficulty. (See Illus. 8-14.) This capability is enhanced when narrower blades are used. A No. 4, 5, 6, and sometimes a No. 7 blade can make zero-radius or "on-the-spot" turns in most wood. Wider blades (Nos. 7-12) will be slightly more difficult to use in wood ½ inch thick and thicker, and will give less desirable results.

As the wood is turned to make a zero-radius corner cut, the blade has a tendency to repeatedly lift the wood off the table on the upstroke, and slam it down again on the downward stroke. In such a situation, the beginner should initially use

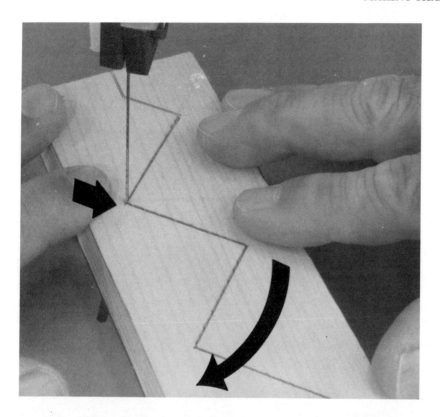

Illus. 8-15. *Making a sharp cornering cut to the right. First, stop the forward feed. Then use your left index finger simultaneously as a pivot point (with downward pressure) and to press the wood against the left side of the blade (towards the right), as shown by the short arrow. Quickly turn the stock, as shown by the long arrow, so that you can proceed to cut in the new direction.*

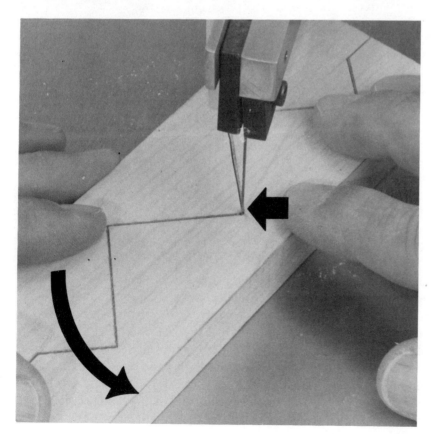

Illus. 8-16. *Making a sharp cornering cut to the left. The right index finger, close to the blade, pivots the wood and holds it against the side of the blade as the work is quickly rotated. As a general rule, apply sideways pressure on the stock towards the right when turning right and towards the left when turning left (as shown here).*

Illus. 8-17. *Making an on-the-spot turn. Cut into the board and stop the feed. In one simultaneous maneuver, apply pressure to the side of the blade (short arrow) while spinning the workpiece around very quickly.*

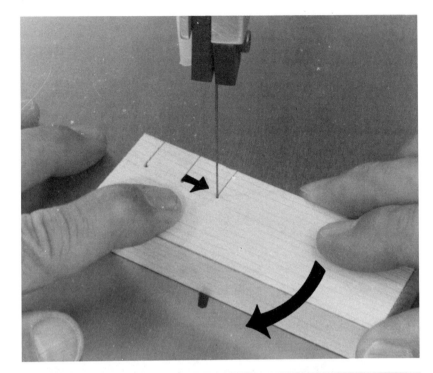

Illus. 8-18. *Continuing the on-the-spot turn. As the stock is spun quickly around the full 180 degrees, shift pressure from against the side of the blade to the rear of the blade.*

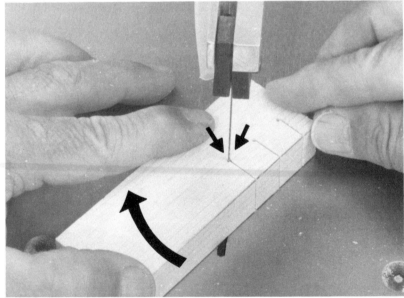

a good hold-down. When he has gained sufficient experience using the saw, he can prevent the work from jumping up and down by exerting physical pressure on the workpiece as he quickly turns it.

The best way to learn how to make a corner cut and on-the-spot turns is by practicing on scrap. Illus. 8-15 and 8-16 show and explain how to cut a right-angle corner in ¾-inch-thick softwood without stopping with a No. 7, 8, or 9 blade. Cleaner

and sharper turns can obviously be made with narrower blades, but it's generally impractical to use blades narrower than a No. 5, 6, or 7 blade in stock 1 inch thick and thicker.

On-the-spot turns are made the same way as corner cuts, except that the stock is rotated a full 180 degrees (or more, if desired). The workpiece is literally spun around on the blade. Practice on-the-spot turns. Cut straight into the wood, and

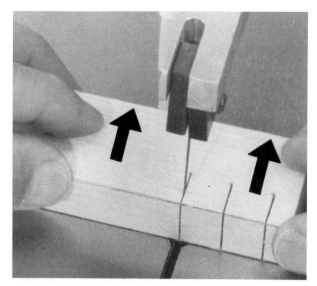

Illus. 8-19. *Completing the on-the-spot turn. The workpiece has been rotated a full 180 degrees around the blade, and now it is being moved so that the blade returns out of the wood on the same path made for the inbound cut.*

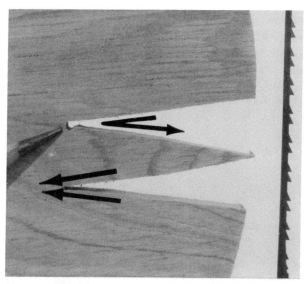

Illus. 8-20. *Two sharp inside angle cuts made with the same No. 11 blade, shown on the right. The upper cut was made non-stop with an inbound cut, an on-the-spot turn, and then by sawing out. The lower cleaner and more precise cut was made by sawing the angle with two inward cuts.*

then spin the workpiece all the way around so that the blade will exit back out of the wood, on the original inbound saw cut. (See Illus. 8-17–8-19.)

Spinning the workpiece around the blade may seem awkward at first, but you'll soon get used to doing it. When you use these techniques on rigid-arm scroll saws and band saws, you have to be much more careful because the wide blades used on these saws can bind in the cut (saw kerf). The spin or full turn is done very quickly on new constant-tension scroll saws. In fact, the more quickly the turn is made, the better.

It will require some practice to develop this skill. However, once you learn to do it with confidence, you will be able to cut sharp corners non-stop when sawing patterns of any profile.

Making Corner Cuts with Wide Blades

The techniques for sawing inside and outside corners and angles are slightly different when you are using wide blades, which are blades numbered from 7 to 12 or any of the wider, less-popular scroll saw or jigsaw blades shown on page **33**. The cornering and on-the-spot techniques used to make sharp inside angle cuts can sometimes result in cuts that are not as clean or precise as expected. (See Illus. 8-20.) In some cases, such as, sawing out large lawn ornaments, this is not essential. In other cases, for example, when making a fine fret-sawn clock that will be viewed up-close, it is essential that all the cuts be perfectly executed.

Illus. 8-21 and 8-22 show how to make perfectly sharp outside corner cuts by making looping cuts in the waste area.

Illus. 8-23 and 8-24 show one technique for making sharp inside corners when you are using a wide blade. It is often easy to cut inside corners or angles that do not have extremely sharp profiles, but cannot be easily turned with the width of blade you are using. (See Illus. 8-25–8-27.)

Illus. 8-21. *Making sharp outside corner cuts by sawing a loop in the waste area (the area of the workpiece that is not part of the pattern).*

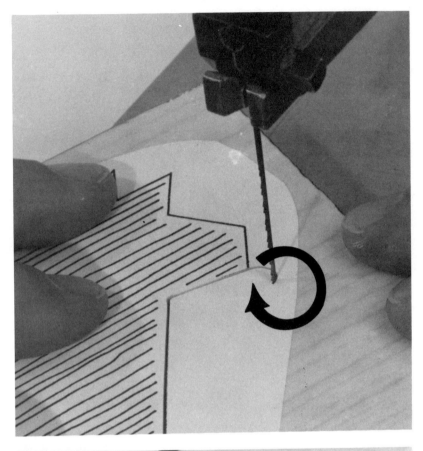

Illus. 8-22. *Completing the looping maneuver. The corner is cut perfectly square, as the cut advances in the new direction.*

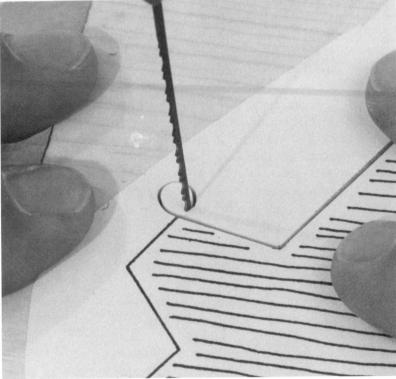

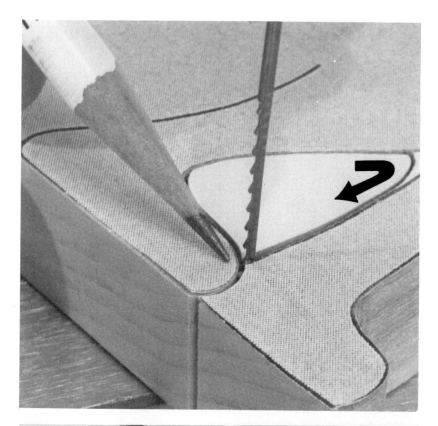

Illus. 8-23. *Looping around this sharp inside angle makes a rough cut that will be "cleaned up" later. Also, note that the cut must be carefully stopped at the previously sawn line. Feed the workpiece very slowly and use good control, to ensure that you don't cut too far as the inside waste piece is freed.*

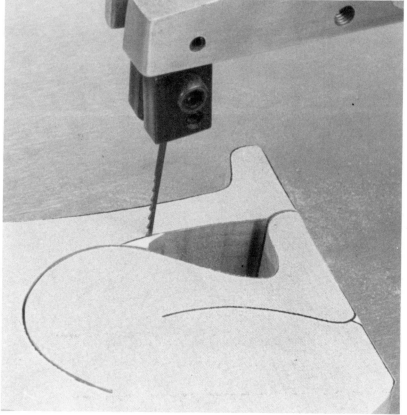

Illus. 8-24. *"Cleaning-up" the sharp inside angle with short, successive cuts.*

Illus. 8-25. *Stop the cut at the inside corner.*

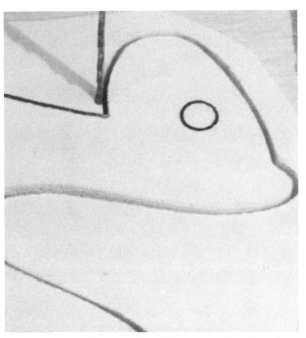

Illus. 8-26. *Back up a short distance and widen the cut, stopping again at the line.*

Cutting Circles and Arcs

Cutting perfect or accurate circles and arcs is a technique that demands a great deal of skill and patience. It is essential that you cut a smooth, uninterrupted curve when cutting circles and arcs. Miscuts inside or outside the line result in "bumps" which will show up dramatically.

Follow these instructions when cutting circles and arcs, or when sawing perfect ovals with inside or outside profiles:

1. Make sure that you have a sharp, fine layout line. If you don't have a good pattern that can be applied onto the wood, make your layout directly, using a compass or circle template. (See Illus. 8-28.)

2. Use the widest blade possible. Make sure that it is sharp.

3. Select a slow saw speed (if possible), for maximum control.

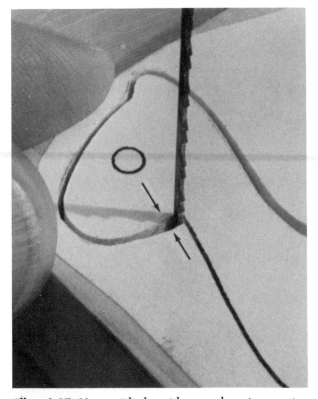

Illus. 8-27. *Now, with the wider cut there is room to turn the stock without twisting or pinching the blade or creating friction which would leave an undesirable charred mark in the corner.*

Illus. 8-28. *Sawing true circles and arcs requires a fine, crisp layout line and a wide, sharp saw blade. Begin the cut by starting in a cross-grain direction, as shown here. Do not cut on the line, but just outside of it; this will save the entire layout line.*

4. Begin the cut in a sawing direction that is across the grain, rather than parallel with the grain, as shown in Illus. 8-28.

5. Do not saw on the line, but cut just very slightly outside of it.

6. Feed slowly, turning the stock steadily and directly into the front of the blade. Be extremely careful when completing the cut. (See Illus. 8-29 and 8-30.)

Illus. 8-29. *When the cut comes around to meet the starting cut, a small nipple may remain, as shown here.*

Illus. 8-30. *Very carefully remove the "nipple" or clean up any irregularity remaining between the start and the end of the cut.*

Sawing Thin Material

Thin material, which includes paper, cardboard, plastic, soft metal, and thin wood, plywood and veneer, usually presents two cutting problems. First, this material can be so quickly and easily cut, it is difficult to control the workpiece with good accuracy when feeding it into the blade. Second, a coarse blade will tear out or rip the edge of the wood fibres near the bottom or exit side of the workpiece, leaving a condition gen-

erally known as splintering or feathering. (See Illus. 8-31.)

One of two things can be done to minimize these problems. First, slow the speed of the saw drastically when sawing very thin material, should you have this option. This will give you better control when feeding the material.

If you cannot use your saw at a slow speed, then thicken the workpiece by supporting it on or between scrap or waste material. (See Illus. 8-32.) Inexpensive waste material used to support workpieces during scroll-saw cutting and drilling to

Illus. 8-31. *A condition known as "feathering" is caused when grain is torn out as the blade exits out of the bottom surface of the wood, as shown by the project on the left. You can minimize feathering (as shown by the project at the right) by sawing the workpiece while it is supported on a waste "backer" or by using blades with reversed lower teeth.*

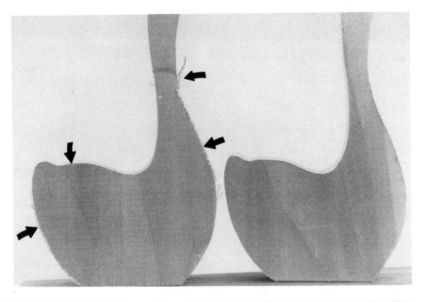

Illus. 8-32. *Sawing thin material that's sandwiched between two pieces of waste material (inexpensive wall panelling). The extra overall thickness makes it easier to control the workpiece when you are feeding it, and the "backer" under the workpiece reduces splintering or feathering because it supports the wood fibres at the cutting area.*

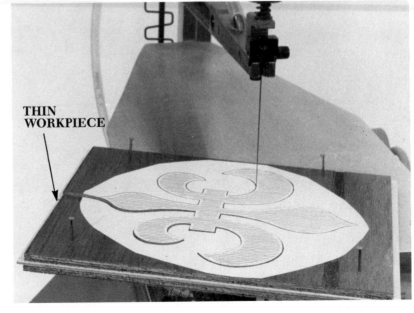

THIN WORKPIECE

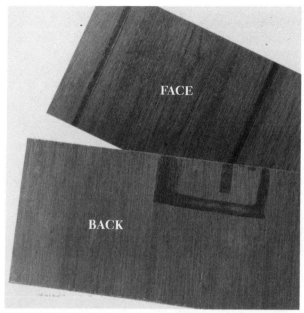

Illus. 8-33. *Scraps of cheap, prefinished wall panelling make good backers and supporting material when you are sawing out delicate and thin objects. This material, in fact, may be useful for sawing out certain projects, and as templates.*

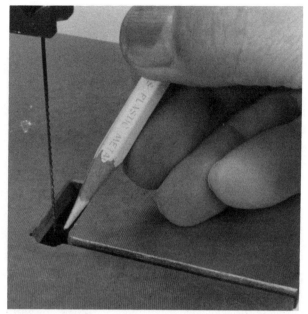

Illus. 8-34. *An auxiliary table placed on top of the regular saw table can reduce the opening around the blade to almost nothing.*

minimize feathering is called "backer." Hardboard, cardboard (such as found in cardboard boxes), cheap plywood, and scraps of cheap prefinished wall panelling are good to use as backers. (See Illus. 8-33.)

Auxiliary Saw Table

The blade opening in the saw table on most saws is large, because a large blade opening is necessary for certain jobs. However, because of this large opening, the saw table cannot provide adequate support under the workpiece near the blade. (See Illus. 8-34.) Illus. 8-35–8-38 show and describe how to easily make an auxiliary saw table that can reduce the opening around the blade considerably. Using an auxiliary table is especially practical when sawing small parts. The auxiliary table closes the opening around the blade where small parts or pieces would normally fall through and might get lost.

Veining

Veining is a very basic sawing technique that adds more character or realism to certain patterns. Veining is simply making a single saw cut (kerf) through the workpiece that makes a visible line that, as a design element, enhances the pattern. (See Illus. 8-39 and 8-40.) This effective technique was named veining by early scroll sawyers when they cut out various leaf patterns and cut in single lines to represent the veins on a leaf.

Sawing Large Cutouts

Some small saws can be used to make large cutouts, depending upon the complexity or nature or the specific pattern. (See Illus. 8-41 and 8-42.) Handling such large pieces and rotating them between your body and the saw blade while maintaining control over the feed can become quite a challenge, especially when you are making small

Illus. 8-35. *Step A. Select suitable sheet material such as 1/8–1/4-inch-thick plywood or hardboard cut about two inches wider and longer than the table on your saw. Make a saw cut from one end to the appropriate spot that will provide an equal overhang all around the saw's table.*

Illus. 8-36. *Step B. Mark the shape of the table all around the bottom of the plywood.*

Illus. 8-37. *Step C. Glue on about three small scraps of wood to serve as stops to keep the auxiliary table fixed to one spot and to prevent it from moving. Note that the table can be removed and replaced again in the exact location at any time.*

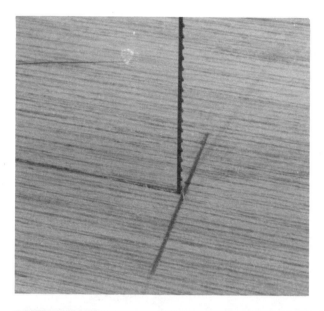

Illus. 8-38. *This close-up shows support all around the saw blade. This is important when you are sawing thin material, very small and delicate cutouts, or material that is susceptible to feathering on the exit side of the workpiece.*

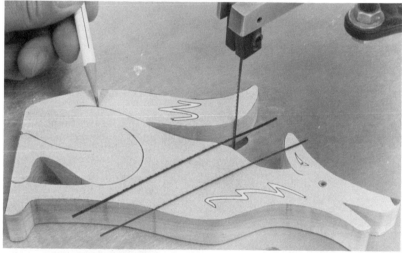

Illus. 8-39. *Basic veining cuts have been used on this project. Incorporated into the pattern design, these cuts define the leg and tail. Cuts such as these will be more visible if heavier blades, which cut wider kerfs, are used.*

Illus. 8-40. *A No. 11 blade is used to cut the outside shape and to make the veining cuts shown. Here the cut has been stopped, and the operator is backing out to continue the outside cutting.*

Illus. 8-41. *Making a very large cutout on a 14-inch saw. Doing quality, precise sawing with cutouts of such sizes can present some special problems. Gradual curves and straight-line work can be handled with a two-handed feed, as shown. Note the use of the hold-down, which is very valuable here.*

Illus. 8-42. *Another way to control the work to help make sharper curves and turns more easily is to feed the work with one hand and use your other hand to pivot the work.*

radius or sharp turns. It is better to make such cuts from a standing rather than a sitting position. If possible, try to reach with both your hands over the table to hold down and guide the workpiece. If that's not possible, use the one- or two-handed feeding techniques shown in Illus. 8-41 and 8-42.

Chapter 9

MAKING INSIDE CUTOUTS

One of the scroll saw's strongest advantages over other power tools is its ability to cut out inside openings. This is a cutting technique that beginners will want to learn early. Also referred to as "piercing" and internal- or inside-cutting, this work involves threading the blade through a hole drilled into the waste area of the workpiece. (Illus. 9-1 and 9-2.)

Some of the basic blade-changing steps explored in Chapter 6 must be performed to saw out each area of inside waste from the pattern. Usually, you have to do the following: release the blade tension, remove the upper blade clamp, thread the blade up through the drilled hole, reattach the blade clamp, and reset the proper tension. These steps can be done much more

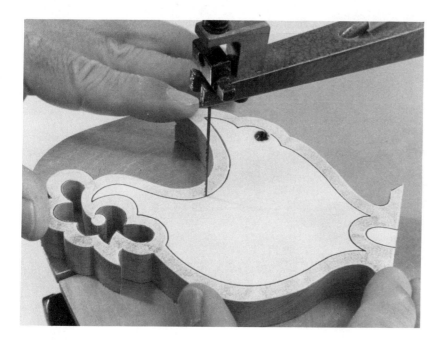

Illus. 9-1. *The process of sawing away the internal waste area from a pattern is known as "inside cutting." Note the starting hole through which the blade was threaded.*

Illus. 9-2. *The inside cutting of hardboard to make patterns and templates for scroll-sawing.*

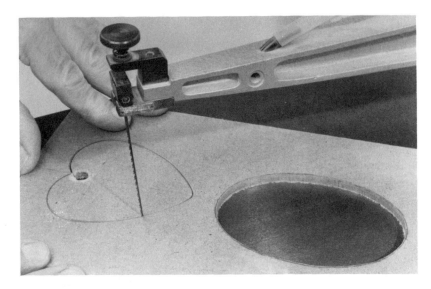

Illus. 9-3. *Basic inside cutting employed to make a name sign.*

quickly on some saws than others. However, it is surprising how practicing these steps will speed up the overall process, and save some time. While saving a few seconds threading a blade may not be important to beginners, it is to fretworkers who cut out projects that sometimes have hundreds of inside cuts. (Fretwork is a scroll-sawn design that is more elaborate and delicate than other scroll-sawn objects, and has many inside openings.) Illus. 9-3 and 9-4 show basic projects on which inside cutout procedures are used.

Drilling Blade-Entry Holes

Use a handheld drill or a drill press with a bit of the appropriate size. The size of the area to be cut away can determine what size bit to use and the number of blade threading steps involved. If the

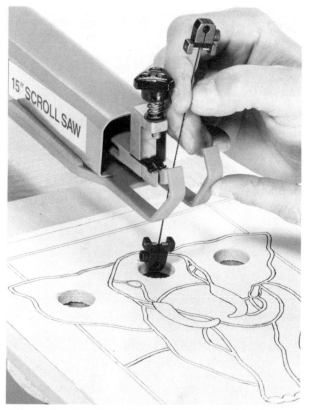

Illus. 9-4. *Inside veining (or line work), which is simply sawing a line through the work, adds greatly to the detail and visual appeal of this fretted angel project.*

Illus. 9-5. *These large holes permit the blade clamp and the blade, assembled together, to be threaded through the workpiece. Smaller inside waste areas will require smaller holes, and only the blade itself can be threaded through the workpiece.*

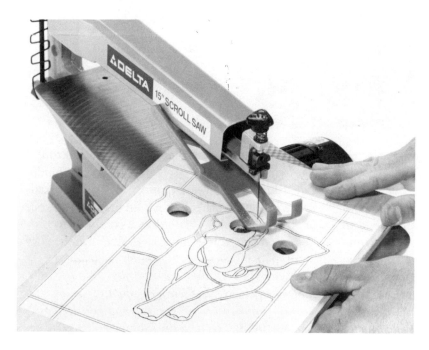

Illus. 9-6. *When the blade clamps are set on the arms and the blade is tensioned, sawing can proceed.*

Illus. 9-7. *Small waste areas will require the drilling of small holes. Note the hole at the right, drilled at the end of the cutout area. Its diameter equals the shape of the sharp curve required.*

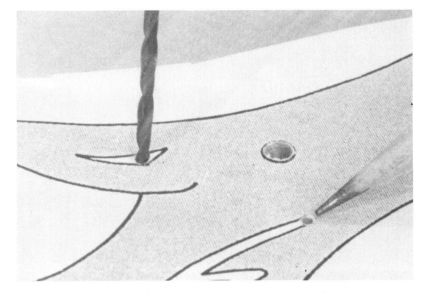

Illus. 9-8. *Sometimes you use the inside-cutting technique on projects that do not have any waste pieces. When making puzzles like the one being made here, and in some inlay and intarsia work, inside parts that are cut free are part of the project. When using inside-cutting techniques on these types of puzzles and for inlay and intarsia work, very small holes must be drilled exactly on the cutting line. It's best to drill such holes at corners or at intersections, as shown here, rather than at some point along a smooth curve.*

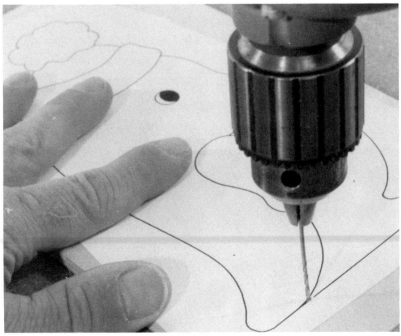

waste area is of sufficient size, it's often advantageous to drill or bore larger holes. They should be large enough to accommodate the blade with the blade clamp attached to it. (See Illus. 9-5 and 9-6.) Drilling larger holes eliminates the need to remove the blade clamps from the blade. However, more often the waste areas are small and dictate small-diameter holes about or exactly equal to the width of the blade. (See Illus. 9-7.)

There are certain jobs where the inside cutout pieces are an important part of the project itself,

such as pieces to be freed from the background when certain kinds of puzzles are being made. (See Illus. 9-8.) In such cases, as well as in advanced inlay, marketry, and intarsia work, very small holes must be drilled to accommodate very small blades. Sometimes you will prefer very small drills, $\frac{1}{16}$ and even $\frac{1}{32}$ inch in diameter.

Whenever drilling blade-entry holes, also called "saw gates," it's important to support the workpiece on a flat scrap backer (piece of scrap). (See Illus. 9-9.) This will minimize splintering on

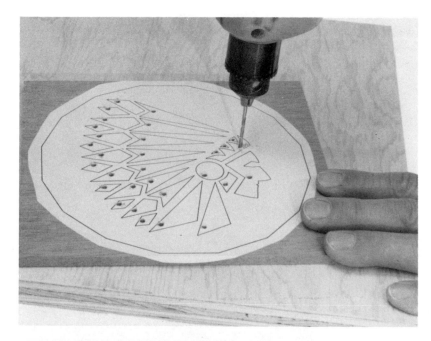

Illus. 9-9. *Holes should be drilled with the work supported on a waste backer board, especially when they are close to the layout lines. This will eliminate or reduce splintering around the hole as the blade exits through the bottom of the workpiece.*

Illus. 9-10. *After drilling all the saw-gate or blade-entry holes, turn the workpiece over and remove any grain tear or existing drilling splinters with sandpaper. This is important, to ensure that the workpiece will lie flat on the saw table.*

the bottom side as the drill bit exits through the workpiece. Just to be sure the workpiece will lay flat on the saw table, it's good practice to lightly sand the bottom side to remove any existing splinters near the holes. (See Illus. 9-10.)

If you have a saw that only carries pin-end blades, you may not be able to cut out small openings like those that can be cut with small pinless fret blades. However, if you have a bench grinder or a fine hand file, you can modify pin-end blades to make them more usable for making smaller cutouts. Simply reduce the width of the blade ends and slightly shorten the pins so that the blades will slip through a smaller hole than normally required. (See Illus. 9-11–9-13.)

Threading the Blade

The exact procedure used to thread the blade through the workpiece will depend upon the overall size of the sawing job at hand and the features provided by the design of your scroll saw. Pick the easiest, quickest procedure and learn to do it as smoothly and as swiftly as possible. As you progress into sawing fretwork, which has a greater number of elaborate cutouts, you will repeat the procedure hundreds of times.

One blade-threading method not suggested in current owner's manuals is shown in Illus. 9-14–9-16, which depict a blade being threaded and the blade and a clamp being assembled on a modified Taiwanese saw. This exact technique can be used on fairly small workpieces with all Hegner saws and other saws that have the Hegner upgrade kit described on page 43. Otherwise, the upper blade clamp has to be secured to the blade while it is held tightly in place on the upper arm. (See Illus. 9-17.)

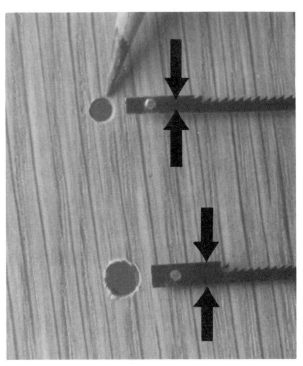

Illus. 9-11. *The modified, narrower (ground) blade end (above) slips through a much smaller hole than the standard untouched blade (below).*

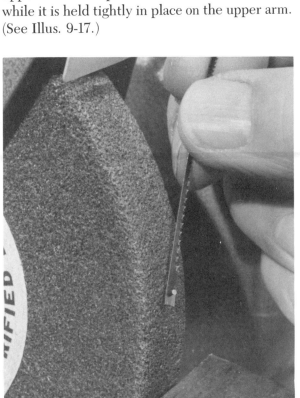

Illus. 9-12. *Grinding the length of a pin on a pin-end blade.*

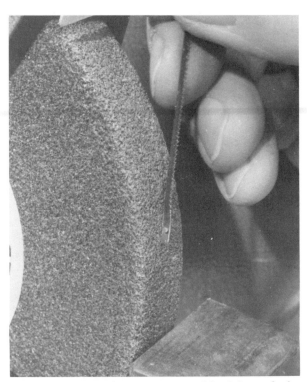

Illus. 9-13. *Grinding down the width of the end of a pin-end blade.*

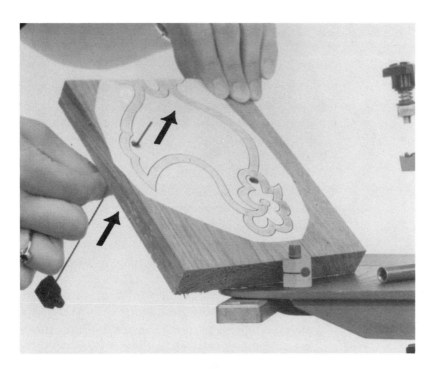

Illus. 9-14. *In one blade-threading method, you first remove the upper blade clamp and then thread the blade through the workpiece from the bottom.*

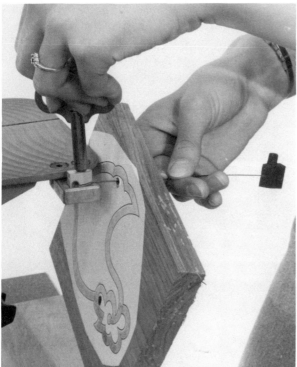

Illus. 9-15. *Next, secure the upper blade clamp to the blade. The features provided by your saw, the size of the workpiece, and the procedures recommended in the owner's manual will dictate how to do this. You can use this technique on Hegner saws or imported saws with a Hegner upgrade kit.*

Illus. 9-16. *Finally, mount the workpiece with the threaded blade assembly to the arm. This is easy to do on saws that have table slots that go all the way to the edge of the table.*

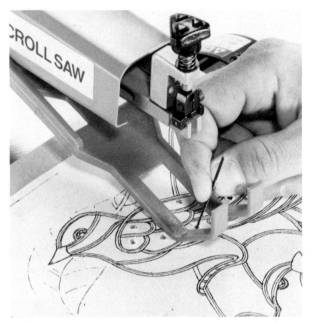

Illus. 9-17. *A slower, less-preferred blade-threading procedure. The upper blade clamp is held tightly in place on the upper arm, with the thumbscrew turned down against it. The threaded blade is inserted into the blade clamp and then tightened with the appropriate wrench or thumbscrew. Each type of saw has its own procedures for threading, clamping, and tensioning the blade. These procedures are explained in the owner's manual for the saw.*

Making the Cutouts

Once the blade is properly threaded, clamped, and tensioned in the saw, proceed to cut. If you normally depend upon the assistance provided by a good hold-down, be aware that it is only effective when it is riding on the surface of the workpiece. (See Illus. 9-18.) If you turn or rotate the workpiece so the hold-down is over a space where a cutout has been removed, the hold-down is of no help.

Square, straight, vertical cuts are important when sawing thick stock. (See Illus. 9-19.) If slanted cuts have been made, the waste will not come out freely from the workpiece, leaving you with an unsolvable problem(s). Always be sure that the table is perfectly square to the tensioned blade.

After some practice, you will be able to cut irregular inside curves (Illus. 9-20), inside straight lines, sharp turns, and severely acute inside angles routinely. Sometimes true, circular inside cutouts are best not sawn at all, but rather drilled or bored. (See Illus. 9-21.)

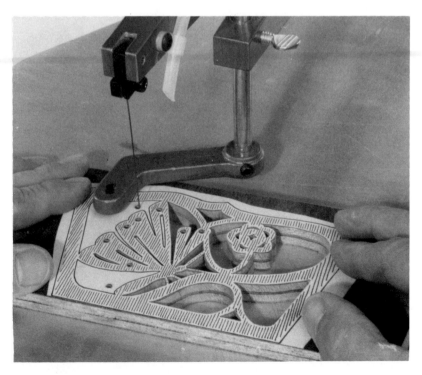

Illus. 9-18. *The hold-down will not be effective when the stock is rotated or turned so that a space where waste has been cut away passes under it.*

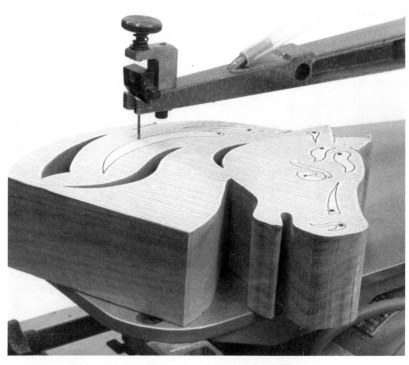

Illus. 9-19. *Making internal cuts in very thick stock. The cuts must always be straight and vertical. Otherwise, the waste will not come out freely.*

Illus. 9-20. *When cutting irregular curves, or any other type of internal cut, saw on the line or just to the inside of it, as shown here.*

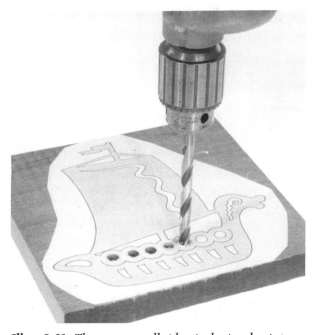

Illus. 9-21. *The seven small, identical, circular internal cutout areas required of this pattern are best drilled or bored. This will provide far more uniform consistency in the size and shape of the holes than could ever be achieved by sawing each separately.*

Illus. 9-22–9-26 show and describe one technique that can be employed to cut away waste areas with very sharp inside angles. This technique can be employed whenever an "on-the-spot" turn and continuing sawing technique is not satisfactory.

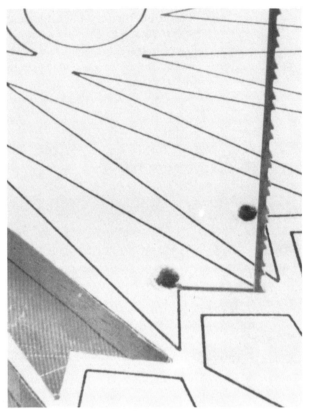

Illus. 9-22. Step A. *Saw from the saw-gate or blade-entry hole to the corner, and then stop.*

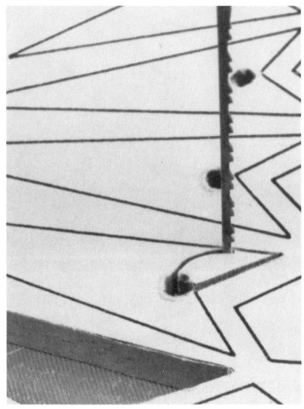

Illus. 9-23. Step B. *Back up a short distance and then make a looping cut, as shown, that will terminate at the same corner.*

Illus. 9-24. Step C. *Remove the little piece of scrap. Rotate the workpiece, backing the blade into the corner. Proceed to saw, by starting at the corner and continuing along the straight line, as shown.*

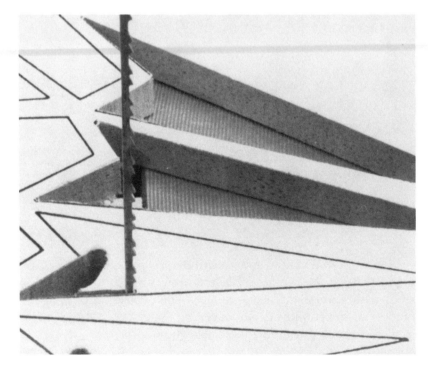

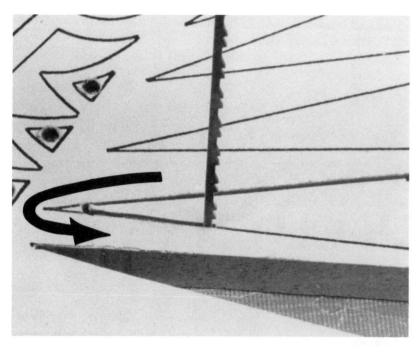

Illus. 9-25. *Step D. If the blade is too wide to make a clean on-the-spot turn, simply round out the corner, as shown, and clean it up later.*

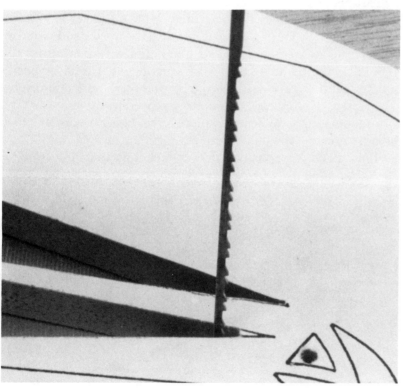

Illus. 9-26. *Step E. Final step. After most of the waste has been removed, clean up the sharp corner by making two short inward cuts, as shown. Make sure that all such cleanup work is completed before removing the blade.*

Chapter 10
STACK-CUTTING

Stack-cutting is the process of holding two or more pieces together, one on top of the other, and sawing them all at once. (See Illus. 10-1.) Some scroll sawyers also call this process "pad"- or- "plural"-cutting.

Stack-cutting saves time and increases production. At least two identical pieces can be cut with about the same effort and amount of time that it takes to cut just one piece.

In addition to making a number of identical parts or pieces all at once, there are other reasons to use stack-cutting techniques. (See Illus. 10-3 and 10-4.) They are helpful when you are cutting very thin material. In such a case, simply "sandwich" the material between two pieces of waste material. (See Illus. 8-32 on page 94.) Stack-cutting is also used when the work is supported on a backer board to minimize feathering on the bottom along the sawn edges. Certain types of advanced marquetry and inlay work also involve special stack-cutting procedures.

Whenever pieces are being stack-cut, they should be fastened together in some way. There are many different techniques, some better for

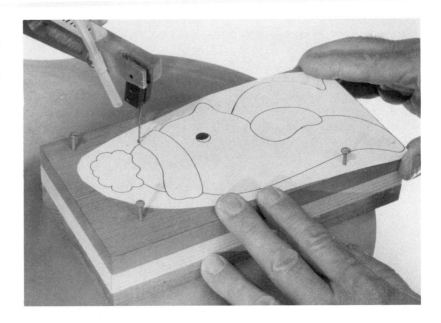

Illus. 10-1. *Stack-cutting involves sawing two or more pieces, one on top of another, all at one time. These three thick layers have been nailed together in their waste areas.*

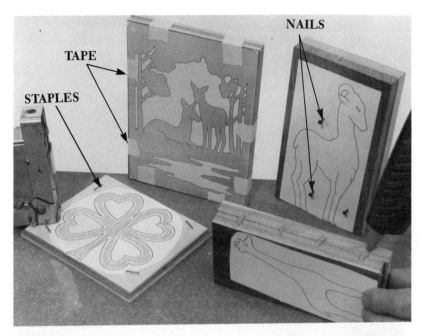

TAPE

STAPLES

NAILS

Illus. 10-2. *Some of the many methods of holding layers of wood together for cutting.*

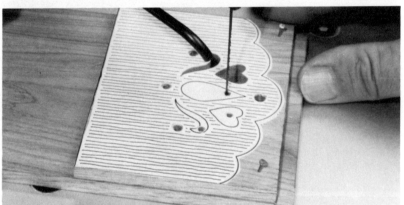

Illus. 10-3. *Many of the basic sawing techniques, including the cutting of inside openings, can be combined with stack-cutting practices. Note that these two parts are held together with small nails that are driven into the waste areas. Obviously, you should make the inside opening cuts before the decorative end cut, which, when completed, will free the layers from each other.*

Illus. 10-4. *The result is two pieces with identical end cuts. The designs of the inside opening cut match exactly the designs of the pattern.*

Illus. 10-5. *Small pieces of double-sided tape hold the layers together for stack-cutting.*

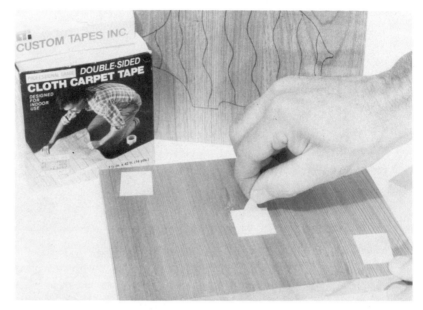

Illus. 10-6. *A drop of hot-melt glue applied to the waste areas (at the corners) is a quick way to hold layers together for sawing.*

Illus. 10-7. *A drop of glue strategically placed within the waste area of each layer is another good way to hold the layers together. The glue is applied between these two previously drilled holes. The holes are drilled through all the pieces as the operator presses them down with his hands against a scrap-board backer.*

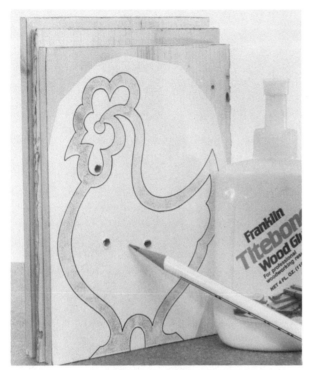

Illus. 10-8. *Just one drop of glue applied between each layer in the middle of these two reference holes holds this stack together.*

certain applications than others. (See Illus. 10-2.) One basic and practical technique—provided the stock is sufficiently thick and there is enough waste area—is to nail or staple the pieces together. (See Illus. 10-1–10-4.)

Sometimes certain projects do not have a waste area. In such cases, you may have to tape or staple along the edges, as shown in Illus. 10-2, or use double-sided tape, as shown in 10-5. Some double-sided tapes have an aggressive adhesive, and you may have problems separating it from thin, delicate cuttings. Use only a small amount of double-faced tape, just enough to hold the workpieces together.

Another way of bonding workpieces together is to spray both surfaces of scrap paper with the temporary-bonding spray adhesive used to mount patterns directly to the work surface, and then insert the scrap paper between two workpieces. This works very effectively on smooth, flat surfaces. The spray-adhesive-coated paper is strong enough to prevent the layers from slipping during sawing, and it can be peeled off easily. This makes it easy for you to separate the layers when you are finished sawing, and there is hardly any adhesive residue left on the surface.

You can also glue layers together with quick-setting hot-melt glue. (See Illus. 10-2 and 10-6.) Regular woodworking glues are also effective in some cases. They set fairly fast, and can also be used to hold layers together in the waste areas. One system for gluing together waste areas of inside cutouts is shown in Illus. 10-7 and 10-8.

Whatever system you elect to use, it will be more effective if you fit the layers against each other without any gaps or openings between. Any gaps or openings will result in feathering or grain tear on supported pieces. Hot-melt glue and small pieces of double-sided tape between layers generally leave gaps more so than nailing or other ways of fastening the pieces along their edges.

The holes for any internal-cutting are usually drilled after the pieces have been fastened together, as if they were one piece. Also, when stacking pieces to a thickness that nears the maximum thickness-cutting-capacity of your saw, make sure that the table is set perfectly square to the tensioned blade. Otherwise, pieces cut from the top layer will be of a different overall size than those cut from the bottom layer. If this happens anyway, you may have a dull blade, have used the wrong blade, or there may be a more serious problem with your saw relating to poor bearings, cheap construction, and/or improper assembly.

Illus. 10-9–10-13 show and explain the stack-sawing procedures used to make two identical sides of a corner shelf.

Illus. 10-9–10-13. *Stack-sawing procedures used to make two identical sides of a corner shelf. Step A. Hold the pattern unbonded to the workpiece to use as an aid in chalking a line for a roughing-out cut.*

Illus. 10-10. *Step B. Sawing the individual layers somewhat diagonally. This divides the board, making two rough-cut pieces that you will stack together to saw a corner shelf.*

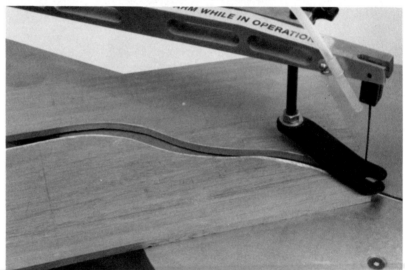

Illus. 10-11. *Step C. Stack and fasten the pieces together with small brads in the waste area. Apply the pattern to the edge of the top piece. Note that the lower piece extends beyond the pattern a distance that equals its own thickness. This ensures that both inside faces will be the same when assembled with a nailed butt joint along this edge.*

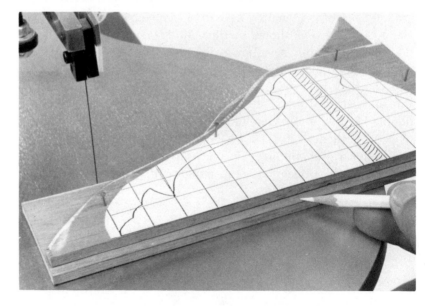

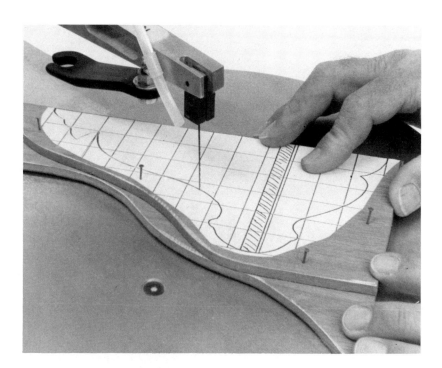

Illus. 10-12. *Cut both pieces with a No. 5 or a No. 7 blade.*

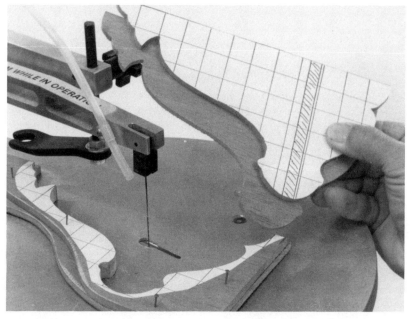

Illus. 10-13. *Both resulting pieces are identically cut.*

Chapter II

BEVEL-SAWING

Bevel-sawing involves any kind of work in which the table is intentionally set so that it is not perfectly square to the tensioned blade. The result is a vertically slanted cut surface. Whether the table is adjusted a full 45 degrees to the blade or merely clamped 1 degree from a true perpendicular plane, the result will be a bevel cut. (See Illus. 11-1 and 11-2.)

When you bevel-saw, you make an inclined edge all along the cutout, be it in a straight or curved direction. Gradual curves and straight-line bevel-sawing are easy and will not present any problems for the beginner. Making square

and sharper inside turns and severe inside angle cuts will, however, create some difficulty. The more the table tilts, the more difficult the cut. The result can be some undesirable inward kerfing at the corners that will nullify a smooth, clean sawn edge. (See Illus. 11-3.) In some cases, it will be better to change the pattern and cut inside corners rounded to an appropriate radius, rather than attempting to make the sharply sawn corners or angles.

Various types of bevel-sawing techniques are used in some areas of advanced scroll-saw work. For example, special joints such as dovetail, flat or

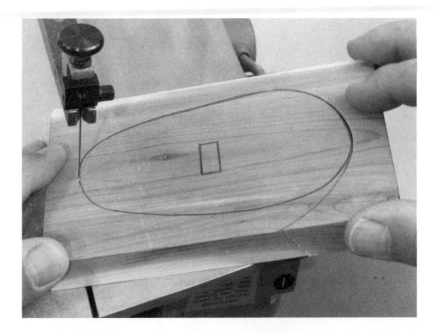

Illus. 11-1. *Bevel-sawing an irregular curve with the table set at 15 degrees makes a slanted edge on this base for a wood cutout.*

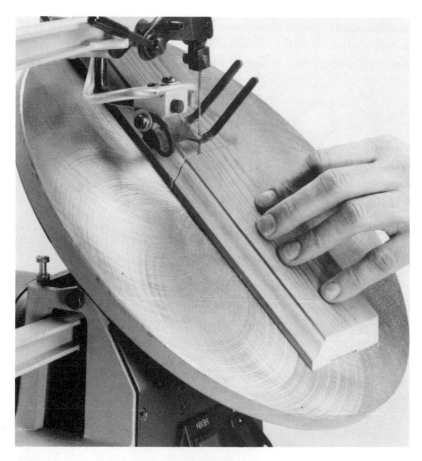

Illus. 11-2. *Straight-line bevel-sawing, with the table set at 45 degrees, is often used for cutting edge mitres, as shown, and making other joints.*

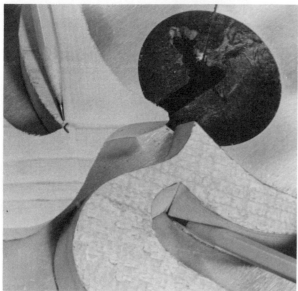

Illus. 11-3. *The results of cutting sharp inside corners when bevel-sawing. The little kerfs cut into the edges (back and front) cannot be eliminated unless the corners are cut on a radius, rather than sharply, as done here.*

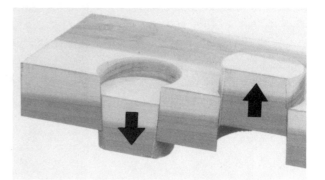

Illus. 11-4. *Slight bevel cuts (3 to 5 degrees) in ¾-inch-thick material make these circular wedge-shaped pieces bind when you attempt to remove them from the workpiece in the directions shown by the arrows.*

edge mitres, and cope joints can be made with some simplicity on the scroll saw. Bevel-sawing can also be used in veneer and solid-wood marquetry, inlay and intarsia, when sawing engraved letters, and even for some forms of bowl-making. Here we will only explore bevel-sawing methods used to make a cutout object stand up in relief from the workpiece background, or to recess it below the surface. This technique can be applied to make some interesting projects such as decorative wall and shelf or desk plaques. As has been explored, cuts made with the table square to the tensioned blade will separate from each other in either direction. When you bevel-cut at even a very slight angle, the pieces will bind. (See Illus. 11-4.) The less the table angle, the farther (higher or lower) the cut piece will move before binding.

There are two other variables that actually determine how far the cut pieces will move before binding: the thickness of the material and the size of the saw kerf (cutting path of the blade). It is, therefore, just as quick and easy to make trial-and-error cuts on stock of a thickness equal to that of your project than it is to try to determine mathematically how to make the cut.

The direction you feed the workpiece into the blade (counterclockwise or clockwise) also determines which surface (the top or bottom) is smaller or larger. (See Illus. 11-5 and 11-6.)

When making cutouts with the table tilted for slight bevel cuts, you can stand the object up in relief or set it back (recess it) from the background. Typical examples are shown in Illus. 11-7. Illus. 11-8 and 11-9 show how to make the actual cuts.

You can make interesting and decorative plaques by combining the techniques of sawing inside cutouts (Chapter 9) with bevel-cutting to set objects in relief or recess them, as desired. You can add a special visual appeal to the project by rounding over some or all of the edges before reassembling the parts. (See Illus. 11-10.)

Illus. 11-5. *Bevel-sawing with the saw table tilted to the left and when feeding the workpiece into the blade in a counterclockwise direction results in a tapered piece that is smaller at the bottom and larger at the top.*

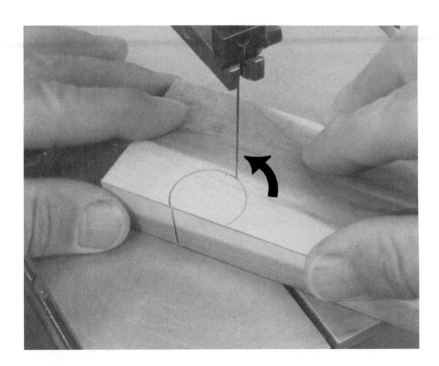

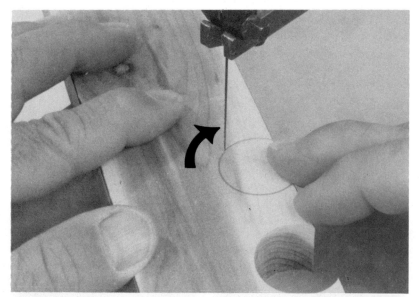

Illus. 11-6. *Bevel-sawing with the saw table tilted to the left and when feeding the workpiece into the blade in a clockwise direction creates a tapered piece that is larger at the bottom than it is at the top.*

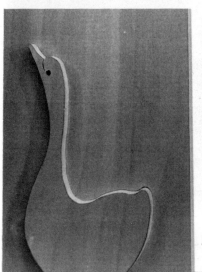 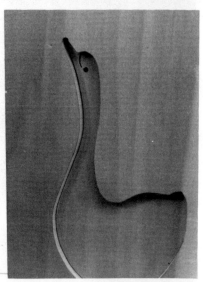

Illus. 11-7. *Bevel-sawing can be employed to make an object stand out in relief from the background, as shown on the left, or to recess (set back) an object into the background, as shown on the right.*

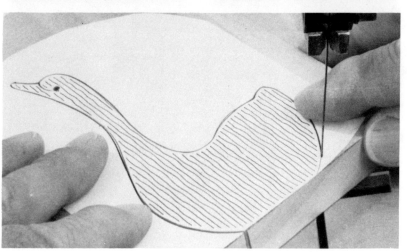

Illus. 11-8. *With the saw table tilted to the left and by feeding the workpiece into the blade in a counterclockwise direction, you can recess the object itself below the surrounding material when you have completed the cutout. The object will be smaller on its bottom surface than on its upper surface.*

Illus. 11-9. *With the saw table tilted to the left and by feeding the workpiece into the blade in a clockwise direction, you can produce a cutout that is larger on its bottom surface than its top surface. This will permit the object to be pushed upward in relief before it binds.*

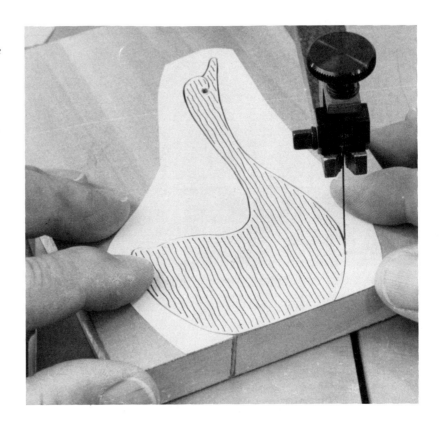

RELIEF

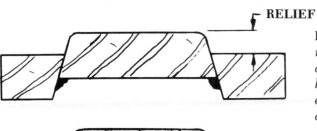

Illus. 11-10. *Two ways to enhance the visual appeal of relief work. As shown above, only the edges of the cutout have been rounded over. As shown below, both the outside edges of the cutout and the inside edges of the background have been rounded. A drop of glue holds the parts together.*

HOT-MELT GLUE FILLETS

Chapter 12
PROJECT PATTERNS

This chapter contains patterns on which you can practice the cutting techniques explored in the preceding chapters. Most of these patterns are usable in their full sizes, as presented here. However, they can be enlarged or reduced to any other size desired easily with an office photo-copy machine. The type of material and the best thickness to use for these patterns is essentially a matter of personal preference, unless specified otherwise.

Illus. 12-1. *Pattern on which to practice straight-line work and sharp cornering techniques.*

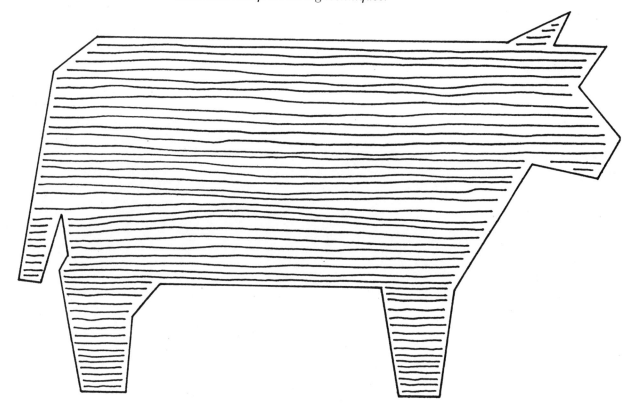

Illus. 12-2. *Little-people and animal patterns.*

Illus. 12-3. *More animal patterns.*

Illus. 12-4. *Angel pattern on which to practice veining techniques.*

Illus. 12-5. *Coyote pattern.*

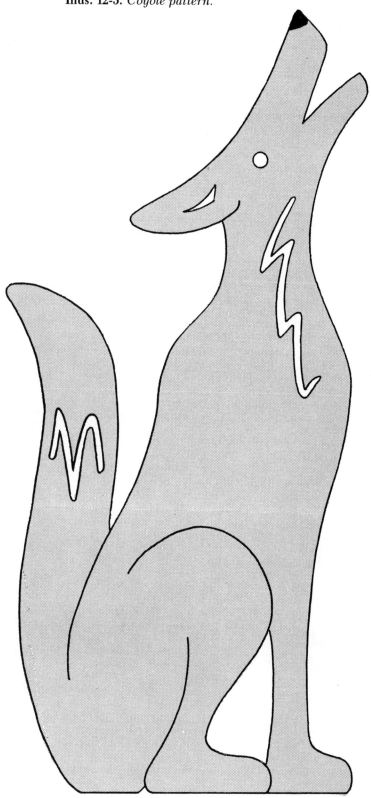

Illus. 12-6. *Penguin pattern.*

Index

Basics Series

Band Saw Basics
Router Basics
Scroll Saw Basics
Table Saw Basics

Other Books by Patrick Spielman

Alphabets and Designs for Wood Signs
Carving Large Birds
Carving Wild Animals: Life-Size Wood Figures
Classic Fretwork Scroll Saw Patterns
Gluing and Clamping
Making Country-Rustic Wood Projects
Making Wood Decoys
Making Wood Signs
Realistic Decoys
Router Handbook
Router Basics
Router Jigs & Techniques
Scroll Saw Country Patterns
Scroll Saw Handbook
Scroll Saw Fretwork Patterns
Scroll Saw Fretwork Techniques and Projects
Scroll Saw Pattern Book
Scroll Saw Puzzle Patterns
Spielman's Original Scroll Saw Patterns
Victorian Scroll Saw Patterns
Working Green Wood with PEG